ORGANIZED RAMBLINGS

{International Version}

HOME EDUCATION FROM A TO Z

Catherine McGrew Jaime, Mom of 12

Other Books by Catherine Jaime

An American Looks at Wuerzburg, Germany
Sharing Shakespeare with Students
Alphabet Fun (with Cheryl and Megan Holle)
Westminster Shorter Catechism Study Set
Da Vinci: His Life and His Legacy

All rights reserved. No part of this book may be reproduced by any means, without permission in writing from Creative Learning Connection, except by a reviewer who wishes to quote brief passages in connection with a review.

Copyright © 2011 by Catherine McGrew Jaime

Creative Learning Connection

8006 Old Madison Pike, Ste 11-A
Madison, Alabama 35758
U.S.A.

www.CreativeLearningConnection.com

TABLE OF CONTENTS

Preface – International Version 1
Preface – Second Edition 3
Acknowledgments – First Edition 5
Introduction, 1st Edition 7
Art and Music 11
Bible and Discipleship 19
Computers and Other Modern Technology 25
Drama, including Shakespeare 33
Encyclopedias and Other References 41
Fun 47
Geography 53
History 55
Indispensable Homeschooling Books, Sites, etc. 61
Jumping Jacks & Fitness 65
Kids (the 4 legged kind) 69
The "Littles" of the Family 73
Multi–level Teaching 77
Nature and Other Sciences 85
Ourselves or with Others? 93
Philosophy of Education 101
Questions and Answers 113
The 3 R's : Reading, wRiting , and aRithmetic 125
Saving Money While Homeschooling 137
Teaching Teens 139
Unit Studies / Topical Studies 151
Vacations 159
Writing it all up (Lesson plans, Record keeping, etc.) 163
X-mas and Other Holidays 165
Yesterday, Today, and Tomorrow (w/Homeschooling) 169
Zoos, Museums, Other Memberships 171
Conclusion 175
Bibliography & Recommended Resources 181
Appendix 183

*Latest picture of our crew, after wedding #3:
Dad, Mom, 7 Sons, 5 Daughters,
and 3 Daughter-in-laws.*

"THERE ARE NO FOREIGN LANDS. IT IS THE TRAVELER ONLY WHO IS FOREIGN."
ROBERT LOUIS STEVENSON

Preface – International Version

As a homeschool mom of over thirty years I have had the privilege of encouraging homeschooling parents in person throughout the U.S. for decades now, and across parts of West Germany when we were stationed there twenty years ago.

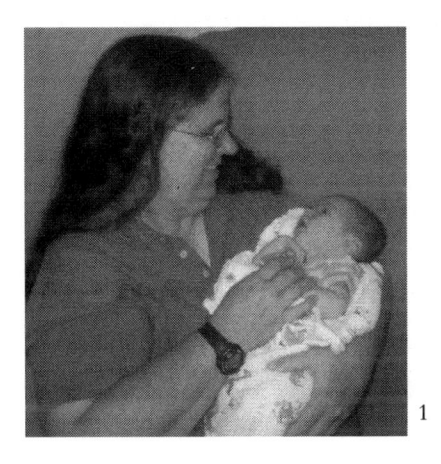

Recently, through the power of the internet I have had the joy of speaking through my written words to homeschool families around the world. I consider it a great honor to be allowed by God to speak words of encouragement to many who are traveling along the path of home educating their own children.

---

[1] Enjoying my granddaughter, Elena.

In the summer of 2011 I traveled to Albania to hold my first granddaughter. While there I had the great joy of being asked to speak about my homeschooling experiences and philosophies to a group of homeschool moms, both Albanian and American. When I shared with those women I realized that while much of what I wrote more than thirteen years ago in the original *Organized Ramblings* transcended country and cultural boundaries, some of it was from a very US-perspective. I have attempted here, in this International Version of the book, to maintain the original setup and flavor of the book, while at the same time modifying some of my "Americanisms."[2]

My prayer is that this book, along with the many others that God has enabled me to write, will be an encouragement and blessing to home educating families throughout the world.

{Any notes added to the book specifically for this edition will be noted this way.}

---

[2] But, good or bad, it will still be a homeschooling book by an American, just as it is clearly a homeschooling book by a Christian!

> "ALL THAT IS GOLD DOES NOT GLITTER
> NOT ALL THOSE WHO WANDER ARE LOST;
> THE OLD THAT IS STRONG DOES NOT WITHER,
> DEEP ROOTS ARE NOT REACHED BY FROST."
> POEM BY J.R.R. TOLKIEN[3]

Preface – Second Edition

The 2009/2010 school year has become a time for me to complete unfinished projects and redo previous ones. After almost 20 years, I was excited to finally redo my first book – *An American Looks at Wuerzburg, Germany*. It was fun to re-read the book after so many years, and it was neat to be able to add pictures to it this time around.

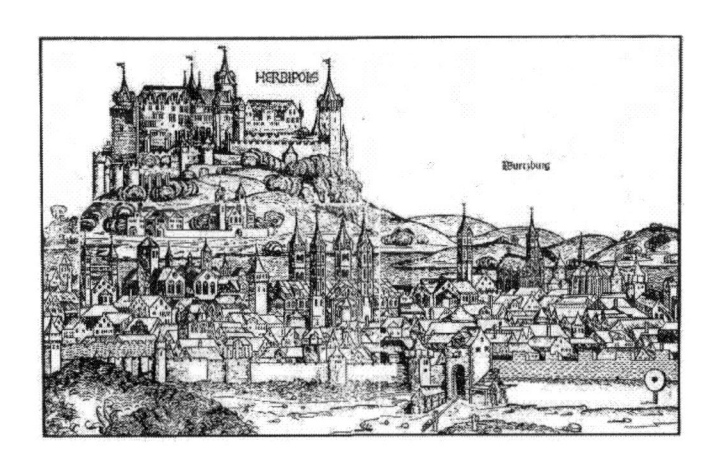

Organized Ramblings was one of the next books I wrote. Of course, things have changed some in our lives since I first wrote it: I've now homeschooled almost **30** years, graduated a total of **nine** of my 12

---
[3] Quoted by Gandalf in *Fellowship of the Ring*

children, added **three daughter-in-laws** to the family, written countless additional books, and started a homeschool resource center.⁴

My three married sons and their lovely wives.

But the more things change, the more things seem to stay the same. We still love homeschooling, we still use many of the same resources, etc. Consequently, I've added numerous pictures to this second edition, but rewritten it only slightly. [In a few places, I've added a new thought, resource, or comment. Most of those will appear in brackets like this, to set them apart.]

---

[4] www.CreativeLearningConnection.com

> "TO EVERY THING THERE IS A SEASON, AND A TIME TO EVERY PURPOSE UNDER HEAVEN."
> ~ECCLESIASTES 3:1

Acknowledgments – First Edition

I want to thank God for His help with this project. I also want to give special thanks to my dear friend Debbie Canida who first inspired me to write this over two years ago. I was on extended bed rest at that time, and was doing a lot of reading as a result. Debbie stopped by to bless my family with a meal and commented to me, "Why don't you stop reading, and start writing?" I took the challenge and spent most of the next month writing out notes on different home schooling topics. The idea of 26 alphabetical chapters came out of the organization of those first notes.

Unfortunately (but all in God's timing!), I lost everything on my main computer when it crashed a few months later. Of course, I was one of the many folks who had not bothered to back up my material. Thankfully, I had hard copies of all my work. I don't trust computers that much! But it was an overwhelming task to re-type all that I had done, so I put the project aside "for a while" – which turned into more than 18 months.

But now, in God's good timing, the completion of this project has finally come. Through the help and encouragement of my sister Cheryl Holle and good friends Vicki Drude and Alison Cox, I have finally had the opportunity to bring this project to closure. Thank you again, Debbie, Cheryl, Vicki, and Alison. This would not have happened without encouragement and help from each of you!

It would also be appropriate to thank my children, on whom so much of this was tried, learned, and practiced. They have been very patient (overall) with me and my husband, as we've learned what works for us and what doesn't, and sorted it all out. And they've even helped me edit the book and make it better! Thanks kids!

> "I WANT TO SEE MOUNTAINS – AND
> THEN FIND SOMEWHERE QUIET
> WHERE I CAN FINISH MY BOOK"
> BILBO IN J.R.R. TOLKIEN'S
> FELLOWSHIP OF THE RING

Introduction, 1st Edition

This is not a "Christian" homeschooling book. It is a book about home education written by a Christian. I make no apologies for my faith, and for my frequent references to God, since He is an important part of my life. If you do not share that faith, you may still benefit from the experiences shared in this book.

Our family, about the time Organized Ramblings was first written.

To Our Family

I have always approached life in an atypical manner. Even in my own schooling days, I was "bucking the system" at an early age – getting in trouble for reading too much in elementary school, taking college classes while still in high school (at time and place when that was uncommon),[5] giving a graduation speech in the form of a story, and the like.

---

[5] I was running out of classes to take by my senior year in high school, so I would go to the high school for one class, sign myself out, drive to the Community College and take two classes, and then drive back to the high school for my last high school class of the day.

This carries over to the way I see education as a whole. I have believed for a long time that **education** is our goal, not **schooling**. My husband and I initially chose to educate our children ourselves because of the failings we had seen in our own schooling. At the time we had never heard of "home educating".

But, please never mistake anything I say as a condemnation of other choices or as an attitude that "this is the only way." That is not my intent. I don't have all the answers; I don't even know all the questions! I will share with you my experiences, my preferences, and my recommendations based on those. Our family has been at this for more than 20 years, and we have learned much and changed much in the process. But what has worked best for us now may or may not be best for your family. Only you can decide. And what works best for us now may not be what works best for us in a few years. Life is, after all, a series of changes.

When I first wrote this, five of our twelve children had moved beyond the walls of our home. It is exciting to see the paths that God leads them on. Don't misunderstand me: They have had their ups and downs too. Ups and downs are a part of life. We can laugh with them and cry with them as they move into the next phases of their journeys through life. One of my older children gave me a note when he was preparing to depart our home – it blessed me greatly when I received it, and even now as I reread it. Among other things he told me, "I have so much to learn. Thank you for teaching me what I know so far." He went on to say, "I thank God that He gave me a mother who I could trust, who would comfort me, and who I could lean on."

To The Home Schooling Journey
I will not mislead you; the journey is not always an easy one. But then, what worthwhile things are? But you can do this, for the sake of your children. You will be a blessing to them in more ways than you can even imagine.

And remember, throughout all of this, our job is not to raise godly **children** – it is to equip our children to become godly **adults**. We are not just educating them, we are raising them, we are discipling them, we are training them.

There is no **one** right way to teach our children at home. Each family must make its own decisions prayerfully and carefully. One of the things that is important throughout it all is balance: balancing school and life, family and others, expectations and reality. Prayerfully work to keep that balance.

I personally have a real aversion to textbooks, which will be apparent throughout the book. Most true learning occurs in spite of, or outside of, textbooks, not because of them. I cringe when I see home educating parents spending so much of their limited resources on a textbook-based curriculum.

But you don't need to do this *my* way – you need to do it *your* way. Home education should be about customizing your children's education as *you* see fit!

To This Book
As I organized my initial thoughts for this book, the idea of an ABC book for parents fell into place. I had started with sections on the topics I've presented in workshops –

Teaching Teens, History, Shakespeare, Unit Studies, etc. I hope this unusual organization method assists you as you read and re-read this book. You may read it in any order that suits you. Each chapter stands alone.

Of course, *my* philosophy of education will be reflected throughout this book. (You may want to read the *Philosophy* chapter for more details on that.) By the end, I hope I will have helped you discover *your* philosophy of education.

My prayer is that this will encourage you, excite you, and motivate you to begin or to continue on the exciting journey of educating your own children. May God bless you and guide you on every step of the trip.

There will be days when it will be frustrating. There are days when we all have second thoughts – but persevere, my sisters and brothers. It's a crazy, but wonderful ride – hang on!

To The Footnotes
Please don't ignore the footnotes
sprinkled throughout the book – I like
to annotate freely, enjoying the full use of "footnotes".[6]

---

[6] According to Merriam Webster's, our favorite dictionary, "footnote" is a "note of reference, explanation, or comment".

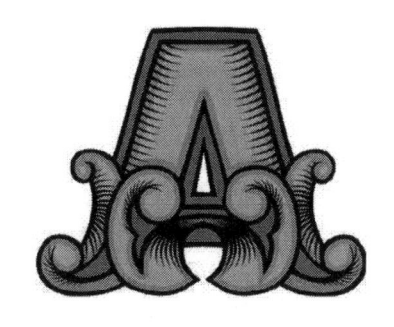

> "O WORLD, AS GOD HAS MADE IT!
> ALL IS BEAUTY."
> ROBERT BROWNING

Art and Music

Too often in our home education journeys Art and Music get relegated to the "study someday" list. In an attempt to replicate the style of the schools we are familiar with (state-run, public schools for most of us), we emphasize the 3 R's (reading, writing, and arithmetic); then there's history, science, and for Christians, of course there's Bible. And as our students get older, we need to throw in PE, Government, Home Economics and on the list goes. It's no wonder that we can teach our children at home for years and we don't get to Art and Music very often!

And how many of us stay away from these subjects because we are so uncomfortable with even the basics? Over the years that was certainly part of my problem.

Consequently, too often during the last 20 years, art and music have been at the bottom of my priority list. Yet, I have often been convicted that I have not given them enough attention and I have been working to restore them to a higher priority in our lives. I do believe that we need to introduce the appreciation **and** use of art and music to all our students.

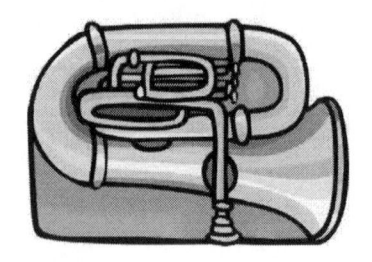

Appreciating Music

I would have to describe myself as one of the many Americans of our day who was not raised with an appreciation of classical music or fine art. I wasn't against these things. I was apathetic, stemming from lack of exposure and therefore knowledge. It wasn't until I started teaching my children at home that I even became aware of my deficiency.

In the last few years I have grown in my appreciation of music with my children. We now enjoy religious music, classical music, Broadway musicals, and much more music together.[7] One of the ways my older children have become acquainted with many types of fine music has been through ushering. They usher for symphonies and musicals several times a year, thus allowing them to taste many different experiences without straining the budget. (In exchange for ushering, they get to attend the programs for free.)

Studying Music

Exposure to music is the first step in studying music. When older family members play an instrument, that certainly helps the younger members. I'm not musically talented, but my husband is. He played the guitar quite often when the older kids were younger. As soon as the older kids showed any interest in music, we saved up to buy a keyboard, and an

---

[7] As long as it's not LOUD music – I still have NO appreciation for that!

electric piano was only a few years behind that. [In 2009, we bought our second electric piano – amazed at how much they have come down in price since we bought our first one almost 20 years ago…But even though the first one was a stretch for us financially, it was a well-used investment.)

We have also found another inexpensive and effective way of encouraging our students in their music: As often as possible, we have found friends and acquaintances that play various instruments, and are willing to share their enthusiasm with our kids. The recorder, piano, flute, and drums have all been introduced that way. With that type of exposure, most of my students have learned to read notes and to play the piano and/or the recorder. Then, as time, interest, and money allow, we set up formal lessons for students who have already shown an interest in an instrument and have already started picking up the basics.

Because I don't have much musical talent or knowledge, we don't have many **formal** music classes at home. Those that we've done have been mainly limited to music appreciation, music history, and very basic music concepts.

In spite of my musical limitations, one of my older sons became musically proficient enough to be accepted into the Berklee School of Music in Boston. In fact, it's probably fair to say, that all 12 of my children are already more musical than I am! Isn't it nice to know that even in this area, our own limitations are not our children's limitations?

Using Music

Music can and should be a part of our lives, even if we are "unmusical". God is a God of Music! Singing to God is mentioned in both the Old and New Testaments. "O sing unto the Lord a new song; sing unto the Lord all the earth...Declare His glory among the heathen, his wonders among all people."[8] and "Let the word of Christ dwell in you richly in all wisdom; teaching and admonishing one another in psalms and hymns and spiritual songs, singing with grace in your hearts to the Lord."[9] And there are many examples of instruments in the Bible: the coronet; trumpet; cymbal; dulcimer; flute; harp; pipe; timbrel (tambourine); and the lyre are all mentioned. Bach said it well in the early 1700's, "The aim and final end of all music should be none other than the glory of God and the refreshment of the soul. If heed is not paid to this, it is not true music but a diabolical bawling and twanging." Do our children appreciate that thought?

Do our children know enough about music to use it to glorify God? In the Old Testament we are given an entire book of praise songs to God – the Book of Psalms. And yet, only recently has my family been introduced to the actual singing of those Psalms in worship to God. What a tragedy that we had missed out on this for so many years! [10]

We can also encourage our students in their worship of God and their understanding of music by teaching them hymns that have stood the test of time. Hymns can give our children such a good taste of doctrine. It was said of Martin Luther that he "did more damage" during the Reformation through the many hymns that he wrote, than through the greater

---

[8] Psalm 96:1,3
[9] Colossians 3:16
[10] We have ordered three different Psalters from Crown & Covenant Publications for use in our psalm singing – all three are wonderful additions to our family worship times.

number of sermons he preached.[11] The history of hymns, as well as the hymns themselves, is an important part of our students' musical and spiritual heritage.

Martin Luther

And of course, not all music must be religious to be valuable. We can enjoy fun songs with our children as part of their daily lives. We can have fun together singing around the campfire or on walks. When our family was in Germany for many years, we had the opportunity to go on hundreds of volksmarches[12] as a family. We would often sing songs just for fun while we were walking, many of them songs that I had learned years ago as a Girl Scout.[13] My kids will often break into song at different times – while riding in the van, or while doing chores, for example. It's really fun listening to "the middle guys" working on chores together, singing in harmony with each other.

And then there are lullabies. My younger children all like having their favorite lullabies sung to them at bedtime. Once when I wasn't feeling well I laid down to rest during the day. My 3-year-old, Sonia, came and lay down next to me. She immediately started singing to me, "Hush little mommy, don't you cry, Sonia's going to sing you a lullaby." She will

---

[11] People would remember and continue to sing the hymns they heard long after they had forgotten the sermons.
[12] Organized, six mile (10 kilometer) walks through the countryside and villages throughout Germany.
[13] A note here – we no longer participate in Girl Scouts in our family, because of the direction that organization has taken.

often make up songs in the midst of playing, also. Now at 4-years-old, she is already learning to sing in parts during family singing times – and memorizes songs much faster than I do!

Music can be a comfort at other times as well. The dying king in Shakespeare's *King Henry IV, Part 2*, cried out: "Let there be no noise made, my gentle friends, unless some dull and favorable hand will whisper music to my weary spirit." May music bless our weary souls, and may it bring us and our children closer to our Lord.

King Henry IV

Appreciating Art
When I think of Art Appreciation, I think of the wonderful examples God has given us in His word. In Ezra we read: "Blessed be the Lord God of our fathers, which hath put such a thing as this in the king's heart, to beautify the house of the Lord which is in Jerusalem." [14]

Beauty is important to God. He appreciates art, so should we! And it starts with appreciating the art that God made in His creation. Do we see this beauty? More importantly, do we share it with our students?

From the beauty of all that God has made we can go on to appreciate the beauty that man has created. Games like *Masterpiece* are a fun way to introduce Art. And visits to art

---
[14] Ezra 7:27

museums, especially when special exhibits are there, add another dimension. When time permits, an in-depth study of particular artists and musicians ("a la" Charlotte Mason) is also good. We studied Monet a couple of years ago – it started as a three-month study. My three-month study turned into the entire school year. By the end, one of my sons was asking, "Is Monet ever going to *die* already?", and another one scribbled on a piece of paper, and then tore the paper into little pieces, informing me that he was "tearing Monet in effigy". I guess you can overdo even a good thing! But, those kids can now spot a Monet painting anywhere!

Claude Monet

Learning Art

Artistic ability should be seen as a gift from God. We have found so far that several of our children are gifted in music and several are gifted in art. We have tried to encourage and support these gifts as much as we can.

While we will not all become accomplished artists, an introduction to the basics is important for all of us. We have used the *Drawing Textbook* by Bruce McIntyre for a great introduction to drawing. It is small, easy to follow, and inexpensive (under $10). We also like the *Artpacs* from Art With A Purpose. They come in eight different levels, from Beginner to Very Advanced. They are also inexpensive at under $6 each (at least a year's worth). Both "curriculums" did a good job of introducing my students to basic art concepts.

When we were using the *Drawing Textbook*, I did the lessons with the kids, and it was fun to see even my limited artistic ability increase. Learning to draw takes time and practice![15] In fact, Leonardo da Vinci would not let his art students go beyond drawing until they were 20-years-old. We may not want to wait that long to introduce other art forms to our students, but it is an interesting thought!

Summary
May our home-educated students be among those Christians who can see the value of art and music – and who desire to glorify God in these arenas. And may we each, as home schooling parents, be willing to go out of our own comfort zones in these important areas.

---

[15] Which is undoubtedly my biggest problem in this area!

"LET US ABOVE ALL THINGS KNOW THE WORD. LET US STUDY IT WITH ALL OUR MINDS, LET US CHERISH IT WITH ALL OUR HEARTS."[16]

Bible and Discipleship

There are two important aspects of the Bible in our homes and home schools: living it and teaching it! The Bible should be the center of our home education, not just an add-on subject that we get to when we can. Many of us are guilty of that, including me! And yet it can and should be central in our education!

Living the Bible
So much of our home educating energy goes to teaching our children their academic subjects. That's a good thing. But at the same time we must not overlook their spiritual training. If we graduate academically prepared students with poor character, we have short-changed our children, and displeased God.

Character training can come in many forms – we can use one of any number of curriculums to help us, or we can rely "simply" on the Word of God. But either way, we must

---

[16] *Education, Christianity, and the State*, pg 22

refocus some of our energy on the hearts of our children, not just their minds.

Even when we focus on character training, I don't believe we will produce perfect children. In fact, we were re-reading the story of Adam and Eve and the Fall recently, and something struck me for the first time: In the Garden of Eden – God was the perfect parent; Adam and Eve were in a perfect environment; and yet they still went astray. They sinned. And it was not because God had failed as a parent.

That was a very encouraging thought to me. We are not perfect parents. Our children do not live in a perfect world. We will make mistakes. They will make mistakes. They will sin. They will fall. And occasionally they will even fail completely. And like our heavenly father does for us – we must pick them up; we must forgive them; and we must continue to love them.

Too many times, parents are blamed when their older children make bad choices. When a young person does drugs or gets involved in premarital sex, parents are seen as failures. We do have a responsibility to disciple them, to raise them and to nurture them while they are under our direct care, and to help them make the right choices. We must guide them; and discipline them; and help them develop the self-control they need. But the time will come when they will go out from under our direct care. They will go into the "real" world. We will pray for them, we will be ready with counsel and help when they ask. But we will need to let them make their own decisions – and their own mistakes. And we must always love them. We cannot earn God's love, and our children should never feel like they must earn ours. And we must remember that we have not failed as parents when our children fail.

We want them to avoid the pitfalls that we know are out there, and sometimes we can help them in that regard, but not always. We want them to grow into the mature Christian adults that we know they can be, without making the big mistakes along the way. And maybe they will…But maybe they won't. If they stray from the path they should be on, we can continue praying for them. And look forward to the day, when like the new, suddenly more mature, king in *King Henry, IV, Part 2*, they say, "Presume not that I am the thing I was."

In the training of our children, there are certainly curriculums out there that will help us build their character. And some of them may prove useful at times. But we have the greatest curriculum in our home already: *The Bible*. "And that from a child thou hast known the Holy Scriptures, which are able to make thee wise unto salvation through faith which is in Christ Jesus. All scripture is given by inspiration of God, and is profitable for doctrine, for reproof, for correction, for instruction in righteousness: that the man of God may be perfect, thoroughly furnished unto all good works."[17]

Sometimes we look too hard in other places for the right Bible study, the right resources, and there certainly is a place for those. But may God help us to see the Bible as the answer to many of those searches. Where do we need to go in addition to the Book of Proverbs to teach our children character? What other book do we need when we have **the Book**? "The Bible, from Genesis to Revelation, presents a

---

[17] 2 Timothy 3:15-17

body of truth which God has revealed."[18] How can it get better than that?

Teaching the Bible as a subject / with other subjects

In 1789, Fisher Ames, one of our first U.S. Congressmen said: "Should not the Bible regain the place it once held as a schoolbook? Its morals are pure, its examples are captivating and noble...We have a dangerous trend beginning to take place in our education. We're starting to put more and more textbooks into our schools...We've become accustomed of late of putting little books into the hands of children containing fables and moral lessons...We are spending less time in the classroom on the Bible, which should be the principle text in our schools...The Bible states these great moral lessons better than any other manmade book."[19] Ames said that 200 years ago! And it rings even truer today!

And earlier in this past century, a great Christian theologian, Gordon Clark, said it this way: "It is an incontrovertible fact that the English Bible has had a greater influence on our language, our literature, our civilization, our morals, than any other book. The children who are deprived of the Bible are culturally deprived, as well as religiously deprived...knowledge of the Bible without a college education is of more value than a college education without a knowledge of the Bible."[20]

The wisdom of both of these men convicts me when I work so hard to incorporate other texts into our school, and don't use the Bible enough!

---

[18] *Education, Christianity, and the State*, pg 16
[19] *America's God and Country Encyclopedia of Quotations*, pg 26
[20] *A Christian Philosophy of Education*, pg 71

Bible: We should be memorizing scripture. (It makes great copywork!)[21] We should be teaching our children the truth of the scriptures and the doctrines we believe. The *Westminster Shorter Catechism* is a great tool for teaching the doctrines of most Presbyterian and Baptist churches, and other denominations have similar tools. It's a shame that the teaching and memorizing of such has gone out of style in most homes.

Literature: In addition to being the backbone of our faith, the Bible is great literature. We need to ensure that our students appreciate that fact. At a secular university, I took a class entitled "The Bible in Western Civilization". It was mainly about the Bible as literature and its impact on our culture. Unfortunately much of our Christian education is missing those important aspects of the Bible!

Geography: In the History and Geography chapter I go into geography more. The key point I make here is that geography should be taught in context! Maps should be a natural part of any history study and any Bible study. Most Bibles even make it easy for us and include the maps right there for us. Let's make sure we take full advantage of those! Do our children make these a regular part of their Bible studies? Can they picture the lands of the Bible in their mind, and follow the

---

[21] The *Writing* chapter has more on copywork.

events across a mental map when they sit in church or Sunday School?

History: Of course, much of the Bible is history. We certainly should not be teaching ancient history or Roman history without incorporating much of the Bible into that study.

Science: The Bible is not written as a "book of science", but where it deals with science it is accurate. We should make sure our students fully understand that! Where the Bible and science disagree, scientists have not yet caught up to the truth of the Bible!

Creation Science is of course intertwined with the Bible, but so are astronomy, and biology, and geology… How can we consider any science with our students, without looking at the Bible in conjunction with that study? And how can we consider graduating our students without giving them the tools to defend against the "scientific" attacks on their faith?

Music: An entire book of the Bible, the Psalms, was written for singing. What a shame that so few of us incorporate that into our schools/homes/churches anymore! Hymns are important, but they should be taught alongside psalms, not instead of them.

Summary
May we each prayerfully consider how to daily incorporate God's word into our home education, and may we each see our children well trained in scripture.

> COMPUTERS ARE USELESS.
> THEY CAN ONLY GIVE
> YOU ANSWERS."
> PABLO PICASSO (1881-1973)

Computers and other Modern Technology

Where do computers and other pieces of modern technology fit into our schools, our lives, our education today? Some see these things as a curse – others as a necessity. I take a "middle road" on the use of most of these items.

Computers
I don't really consider computers useless, but I can see Picasso's point.[22] Computers are useful tools. There are many educational games and curriculums available for computers, but I still prefer not to use most of those (even after 12+ years with one or more computers in the house!). As useful as they are, I just don't like the idea of family members spending great amounts of time in front of a computer screen. Children need more interaction with real people, not machines.

---
[22] Even if I don't care much for his art!

Besides, I don't need any more competition for the available computer time. My students use them to practice/learn typing, and for word processing, for doing occasional emails, and even occasional research, but generally that's it. When they do write with a computer, I allow them to use the spell checker. It doesn't correct all of their "spelling woes", but it certainly helps with many of them.

Bandit "helps" me with one of my writing projects on my latest laptop.[23]

Consequently, I use the computers much more than they do – to keep track of school records, to make our own curriculum, etc. I would not want to be without a computer in our home educating because of how much I use it! [In the last ten years we've added numerous laptops to the mix – I'm on my third – but in our house, computers are still primarily used by me!]

Digital Cameras
One of my recent "technological" purchases was a digital camera. I bought it last summer out of frustration with the cost and hassle of buying, processing, and dealing with film and pictures. One of the unexpected benefits has been that my younger children have taken an interest in photography. Without the additional cost of wasted pictures, it's easier to

---

[23] [I've written several books in a travel series, *Horsey and Friends*. Bandit has accompanied me on two trips to Washington, D.C. and "helped write" those two books.]

give them the leeway to experiment. We just go back and delete the mistakes. In the process my eight-year-old, Victoria, and ten-year-old, Karisa, have both taken some really good pictures. And in the first year we took over 3,000 pictures with the camera. Some of those have been printed and now hang on our walls, some have been emailed to friends and family. Most of the rest are enjoyed regularly on our "personal screen saver" on the computers. [Digital cameras have come down in price so much now that we own several – not counting the ones on most of the cell phones!]

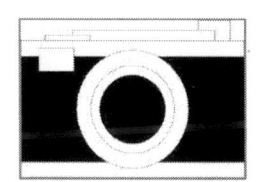

TV

We have been full circle in this area. We went three years without a TV at all, and I threaten to go back to that lifestyle occasionally. But I like the freedom to watch educational videos, an occasional educational special, and the old movies my family is so fond of. Some of my older kids think classical movies, musicals, and Broadways are the only good excuse to have a TV/VCR; while my middle sons think the History Channel and Sports are the real reason for this "necessity". So, all in all, while I will continue to seriously limit its use, the TV is likely to stay around our home – at least as long as the VCR or DVD players work!

VCRs/DVD Players

Since my primary reason to have a TV is to be able to watch DVDs and videos, these are of course essential. We like the quality of DVD's, but I'm a long way from being willing to give up my VCR. For one thing, I have yet to figure out how to edit a DVD! So the VCR stays too. [And after many years, we still have the VCR!)

TVG & Screenit

Since we have not managed to rule out video/movie watching completely, there are two related resources that I find almost indispensable:

> 1) TVG (Television Guardian). This wonderful devise connects between your TV and DVD/Video players. I even found a TV/DVD player for sale at Wal-Mart that included the TVG! This device ties into the closed caption feature of shows and movies and "catches" the foul language before it actually pollutes our ears. As long as the closed captioning is accurate, the bad language is removed. It has made a BIG difference in what my family can watch and enjoy.
>
> 2) www.screenit.com My first preference would be to screen all movies personally, before my kids see them, but that's not practical. This website is the next best thing! My kids know not to even ask about seeing a movie, unless I can get to the computer to "screen it" at the same time. If you want to know the amount of sex, violence, and bad language a movie contains, I haven't found any place better to go.[24] And a word of warning to any who haven't already figured it out – the standard rating system is becoming more and more lax. There are very few PG-13 movies anymore that I

---

[24] [Of course now there are many similar sites. I highly recommend finding one you like – and using it whenever necessary!]

deem acceptable.[25] In fact I was watching a PG-13 movie one evening with my sister and my 25-year-old daughter. I had forgotten to screen it, since it was just us three women. I was mortified at what my single adult daughter saw in that movie, and at the idea that this was a movie aimed at teenagers!

Answering Machine

This may seem a bit out of place with the above items, but it is technology after all. And as a busy home schooler, it is another one that I wouldn't want to be without. Wade Hulcey (husband of one of the authors of the KONOS materials), writing about telephone callers, summarized my position quite well: "Their immediate problem is not our immediate problem." That's exactly why I have an answering machine. I will admit to using this machine as I see fit – not necessarily as others do. I often keep it on when we're home, and then turn it off when we're away from home! That way I have fewer phone calls to deal with during instruction, and fewer messages to deal with when I return home! My apologies to those who have trouble catching up with us – but I find the telephone to be such an invasive devise if I don't find ways to manage it.[26]

---

[25] These days there actually seem to be more *acceptable* R rated movies than PG-13 ones.! Not all R, of course. But many R movies actually have less sex (often none) than the PG-13s aimed at teens! I have on many occasions rejected PG-13 movies, and allowed an R instead.

[26] Which is why people who are trying to get in touch with me do better typically with email then with the phone, but I'm getting ahead of myself…

And this is where this chapter originally ended, until my oldest son read over it and asked: "What about important items such as cell phones/PDAs/ and the internet?" So read on, and we'll get to those:

PDA's [and Blackberries]

Where would I be without my PDA? It was a Christmas present from my husband a few years ago, and I love it for keeping my schedule straight, and for keeping addresses and phone numbers handy. I don't use it for writing as much as I thought I would. I had to upgrade to a laptop for that. [My PDA was soon replaced by a Blackberry – which functions as both my cell phone and organizer – and, to my surprise, regularly as a camera as well.]

Cell Phones

Cell phones and pagers are clearly not critical items for most families. But I will say that both have helped us immensely. With them I can run to the store, or even a Moms' Meeting, and know that my kids can get in touch with me if the need arises...Because my time is limited, and I always seem to have folks waiting for a phone call from me, my cell phone allows me to get much of that out of the way before I get home. [It was almost funny to read what I had written almost a decade ago on cell phones. They have certainly become a part of our everyday lives since then. I can no longer think of any adults I know without them, and in our family, all by the 11-year-old currently have them...]

Email and the Internet [+ Facebook, Twitter, Blogs…]

These should probably have been up there with computers, but I didn't think of them originally. The internet gets a bad rap sometimes! And it certainly is not totally undeserved. But when it comes to research, it's hard to beat the internet. One way we've controlled its dangers is to limit access to the adults in the family. All "non-adults" have to go through one of us to access the internet, making it easier to keep the good, and control the bad. Another family I know only lets the kids on to do internet in pairs – which is also a good tactic.

Email has been great for keeping in touch. We gave up on regular letter writing years ago; email makes us accessible to each other again. We really appreciated email when our oldest son was in Albania for two years as a missionary. It made keeping in touch with him so much easier. And another son is now in France. Again, email is invaluable.

[Again, the changes in almost a decade….Who doesn't do email anymore? The bigger questions today become, what about networking groups such as MySpace and Facebook? I think those are struggles we all go through as parents – how much is too much? I'm the only one in my bunch that does Twitter, so that one isn't hard. I like it for the political communication most of all. And I seem to be much more interested in reading and writing blogs, so that is another area that has become a big help for ME.]

Final Thoughts

As much as we use and enjoy technology in our home, we can certainly live without it when we need to. In fact, my younger children cheer when we lose our electricity. Twice in a two-week period we lost electricity. They were unhappy when it came back on – they were enjoying the adventure without it. Not that we would want to live that way all the time if we have a choice, but it's comforting to know that we can amuse ourselves without the help of technology. In fact, several years back we lost electricity for three days, and it was only the adults who were terribly inconvenienced by the experience! We have pictures of the kids reading and playing games by lantern light. They never once complained about having nothing to do.

It is important to me that my children not need electronic playthings to occupy their time. I decided years ago that "game boys" and video games would not be allowed in our home.[27] Those items have to be among the top reasons that most children today have such short attention spans. Mine do not! They still have their fair share of problems, but short attention span is not one of them.

---

[27] The kids still have access to those types of things at friends' houses, which is more than enough!

"ALL THE WORLD'S A STAGE, AND ALL THE MEN AND WOMEN ARE MERELY PLAYERS: THEY HAVE THEIR EXITS, AND THEIR ENTRANCES, AND ONE MAN IN HIS TIME PLAYS MANY PARTS." [28]

Drama, including Shakespeare

Drama

Are all children born with a dramatic flair, or are mine unusual? My bunch has certainly not lacked for an interest in drama of many kinds. The younger ones regularly "dress up" and choreograph their own dances and plays for us. Our family has been enjoying "plays at home" for decades now.

---

[28] Jaques in Shakespeare's *As You Like it* – not quite our philosophy in life – but a good lead into drama!

A number of years back, my oldest son started a High School Drama Club when my oldest three were in High School. More recently, three of my middle sons have had parts in more than 20 community theater productions, which has given the rest of the family an excuse to see dozens of local theatrical productions. And then at family camping events, at scouts, and at special teen events, there have been great opportunities for the kids to "ham it up".

If drama is not already a part of your life, I encourage you to look into it. There are so many ways to add this new dimension to your home education program. We found Community Theater very easy to get involved in. They're always looking for folks to help with sets and lighting, and even small parts.[29] In our area home educated students are becoming a bigger and bigger part of the Community Theater circle.

It would only be fair to end this section with a word of warning though. Like animals and organized sports,[30] theater can quickly take over your schedule. It would be a good idea before you get involved to determine the limits you want to set – and how involved your family will become. Once you open the door to drama, it's a difficult door to close again!

Shakespeare

I read recently that drama is the most efficient of all the Visual Arts – since it must tell a complete story in a short amount of time.[31] And Shakespeare was a master of drama –

---

[29] The third "serious actor" in the family started his community theater career with a bit part in his first play, and a starring, award winning, role in his second.
[30] See the *Kids* chapter and the *Jumping Jacks* chapter for more information on these!
[31] *Shakespeare Plain* by William G. Leary (McGraw-Hill paperbacks, copyright 1977)

he had to tell a story to an audience using very little in the way of props and special lighting (unlike much of today's "drama"). Shakespeare had to rely on the power of his words – and they are indeed powerful.

Perhaps that's what draws my family to drama in general and Shakespeare specifically – "words, words, words,..."[32] powerful words.

In fact, we've become a bit fanatical at my house when it comes to Shakespeare: we currently have dogs named "Comedy" and "Tragedy", and a fish named "Shakespeare".[33]

I first came across the idea of teaching Shakespeare to my students when I joined a Charlotte Mason discussion list a few years ago, about the same time my fourth child was expressing the desire to "do more Shakespeare". Not having much personal knowledge of or experience with Shakespeare it was a daunting task at first, but one that I was willing to tackle.[34] Not being one to do such things half-heartedly, I jumped in with both feet. Three years later I am probably more enamored with Shakespeare than the son who introduced me to the idea in the first place!

---

[32] Hamlet in *Hamlet*, while pretending to be reading
[33] The fish is a recent addition, the dogs have actually been with us for 5 years.
[34] I've written an entire book on my experiences and suggestions for this, *Sharing Shakespeare with Students*. This is the short version.

A friend asked me awhile back, "Why Shakespeare? Why do we study him? Why do we study his plays?" He lived hundreds of years ago after all. And there are many other playwrights who came before and after that we pay little attention to. Why does Shakespeare deserve so much attention? Mainly because his plays are such a part of our life. Our expressions, even our vocabulary, owe much to William Shakespeare. Entire books have been written on his contribution to the English language.[35]

Shakespeare is also good literature – well written, with good character development, and it is actually a lot of fun to read and watch. And while I have no reason to believe that Shakespeare was a Christian – he was certainly influenced by Christian ethics – which show up clearly in most of his plays.

We decided very quickly that Shakespeare plays were not intended to be read silently (at least not early on in the "Shakespeare experience") – they're meant to be heard and seen. So we have done most of our studies through reading the plays aloud, and watching quality videos (or in some cases, edited versions of the not-so-quality ones!). Libraries usually are a good place to start, and video rental stores typically carry a few. I finally started buying most of the ones we watch, so that 1) I could edit them easily and 2) we could watch the good ones more often. Even my much younger kids enjoying watching them, especially the comedies, so I get my money's worth.

Live productions are also good: high schools and local acting groups often do at least a couple of Shakespeare plays each year. In Northern Alabama we also have Shenandoah Shakespeare Express every March and the Alabama

---

[35] There is something empowering to kids (and adults) when they KNOW where something comes from – when they hear a phrase and know its origin and its context.

Shakespeare Festival in Montgomery, a reasonable drive from us.[36]

But as good as it is to see the plays, it's even better to read them aloud. Well, the *best* is to do both – watch and read! We have done this with just the readers in our family (remember, though, that I had six readers at the time!), with one other family, and with as many as 16 teenagers. Now there is a sight to behold: 16 teenagers watching, reading, discussing, and *enjoying* Shakespeare plays! For us this usually works especially well with students age 12 and up.[37]

Our usual procedure (not the only way, but the way that works well for us):

- We introduce a play one week (typically with a video). Since our class sessions are two hours long, some versions can be seen at one setting.[38]

- I pass out the parts to the students (who's reading what character).

- The next week or two we read the play aloud.

---

[36] SSE is very good – although they do push the "raunchy" elements to the limit sometimes. We've only seen one play in Montgomery, and it was exceptional!

[37] My 12-year-old son has been in our Shakespeare class since he was 10 1/2, but that was really on the young side. He certainly gets more out of it now than when he started.

[38] If I could get families to arrive earlier – I would actually do a 2 ½ hour class, instead of a two hour class, but we just can't work that into our lives at this point – so we make do with the two hour blocks of time. [Actually, we've since changed to a 1 ½ hour class, which works into our schedule better now – so there is no "perfect" class time for this!]

Sometimes we stop there, other times we watch another version. When we have a chance to watch a video again at the end, that's ideal, because then we know the play even better when we watch it.

In other words, in an ideal situation, we would
 1) Watch a play first – to give us the "big picture".
 2) Read it – to see the details.
 3) Watch it a second time,[39] to put it all together.

Time and resources don't always allow for all three steps, but they make a good target.

I find that the comedies are the easiest to start with. Shakespeare's tragedies are also good. Histories are typically the most difficult to understand.[40]

Please do your students a favor – don't make them over-analyze the plays they study. While a basic knowledge of the setting, especially if it's a historical play, is a good idea – we still don't need to pick apart every piece of it. If we don't understand every line we read, that's okay. [41] If we miss something the first time we read or watch a play, that's fine. On the next go-round, we'll pick up even more.[42]

I rarely ask my students questions – In *Hamlet*, I asked a couple of questions like: "Did his mother know what her

---

[39] The same version, or another version of the same play.
[40] For our class, we try to alternate between the three types: Comedy, Tragedy, History, Comedy...
[41] One class period when we were reading *Hamlet*, one of my older students read a very long passage. She finished, look at me, and asked, "What did I just read?" I answered, "I have no idea." We all laughed, and went on.
[42] We've already done several of our favorite plays a second or third time – that was fun.

husband had done?" "Was Hamlet really crazy, or just pretending?" A few thought-provoking questions suffice to make sure they're paying attention.

Recommended Plays

Comedy	Tragedy	History
Merchant of Venice	*Hamlet*	*Richard II*
Much Ado About Nothing	*Julius Caesar*	*Henry V*
Comedy of Errors	*Othello*	*Richard III*
Midsummer Night's Dream	*King Lear*	
Taming of the Shrew		

Quotes – How Many of These Do You Recognize? How many would your student(s)?

From *Hamlet*:
- "To thine own self be true." (Polonius)
- "To be or not to be, that is the question…" (Hamlet)
- "Frailty thy name is woman" (Hamlet)
- "Give every man thy ear, but few thy voice." (Polonius)
- "Brevity is the soul of wit" (Polonius)
- "Something is rotten in the state of Denmark" (Marcellus)

From Other Shakespeare plays:
- "Beware the Ides of March" (Soothsayer in *Julius Caesar*)
- "The course of true love never did run smooth." (Lysander in *Midsummer Night's*)
- "He hath eaten me out of house and home" (Hostess in *Henry the Fourth, Part One*)
- "Friends, Romans, countrymen, lend me your ears!" (Mark Antony in *Julius Caesar*)

- "A Horse, a Horse! My Kingdom for a Horse!" (King Richard in *Richard the Third*)

In Conclusion

Shakespeare has something for everyone. We can see him in our "mind's eye".[43] My avid readers have been known to read or re-read a Shakespeare play "just for fun". But he appeals even to those who are not avid readers. One of my nieces does not particularly like to read – but she loves Shakespeare. She had the part Juliet (in *Romeo and Juliet*) for a recent set of classes – and she read and re-read her lines for the classes. She even borrowed a copy of the play one afternoon, and "snuck off" with another cousin to read it.

Needless to say, my teens[44] may seem unusual in this regards, but I don't believe they are. They're just normal teens who have been introduced to Shakespeare in a fun, and consistent way.

I will admit to "editing" Shakespeare slightly as we go through his plays – we try to skip over the serious sexual innuendos, and I skip the sex scenes that have been added unnecessarily to many of the newer videos, which is why I make it a rule to preview the videos *before* class! But with a little work on my part, we've been able to enjoy almost 20 Shakespeare plays at this point.[45]

If you haven't already, I would strongly recommend "Sharing Shakespeare with *your* students".

---

[43] Hamlet said that to Horatio in *Hamlet*.
[44] And I include the dozens of teens who have enjoyed our Shakespeare class with us over the years.
[45] [Actually, since that point we've done ALL 38 Shakespeare plays – many of them over and over again!]

"OH THIS LEARNING, WHAT A THING IT IS..."
~GREMIO, IN THE TAMING OF THE SHREW

Encyclopedias and Other References

Encyclopedias

When I first read Ruth Beechick's book, *You Can Teach Your Child Successfully*, she quickly became one of my favorite home education authors. In fact, as I read the book, I found only one area of disagreement with Dr. Beechick: her position on encyclopedias; she stated that encyclopedias are a waste of money, and a waste of space on a bookshelf. She based her claim on the premise that encyclopedias cannot cover a subject in depth, but only superficially, and are therefore inadequate.

Well, "I wish to set before you"[46] another way of looking at encyclopedias. In my opinion encyclopedias are indispensable to a family. While I'm all for real books, and for studying a subject in depth (why else would my personal library contain thousands of books, often with a shelf or more on a particular topic) there are times when just a *little* information is all you need or want. And a good set of encyclopedias is often just the place to get that information.

When I know my family has an interest, we soon have books by the dozens on that subject. But oftentimes a question comes up on a "new" subject, and we go straight to the encyclopedias to find the answer.

Encyclopedias have been great when we wanted to see a quick map of a particular country or state; when we've wanted to know who was President at a certain time in our history; or which King of England lived when…You get the idea. [Of course, these days, its often faster just to "google" something on the internet, or to check it out on Wikipedia, but we **still** refer to our encyclopedias often!]

We had a decades-old *World Book* set for years ($25 at a yard sale). We enjoyed it, referred to it, and the younger kids thumbed through it often. It was well worth the shelf space it took up. And after many years with it, I finally decided that a new set was a worthwhile investment. We've never regretted that decision. It may have been hundreds of dollars -- but the hundreds of hours of usage tell me that it was well worth it. And now both sets sit on prominent shelves in my Family Room – and both sets get frequent use. In fact, in the midst of a recent research project, I decided to see what the encyclopedias said about something I had already studied in

---

[46] A quote from the movie *The King and I*.

depth. I was dismayed to find the 1967 article better than the one from 1991.

One other complaint about encyclopedias is that they get outdated so quickly. We did find some occasional frustrations in that area with our first set, but not often (history doesn't often become outdated, much geography doesn't change, and even quite a bit of science remains the same from year to year). With the investment in our new set, we decided to keep it current by buying the yearbook available for every year. Yes, it costs us $30 each year, but hey, ordering pizza for my family costs me $30 or more, and the enjoyment from that is gone in less than an hour! Every year when the yearbook is due in, my older sons anxiously await its arrival. Once here, it is the subject of much attention -- and an investment that brings many more hours of enjoyment and education.

Computer Encyclopedias

Before we move on to other reference books, a few words on encyclopedias for the computer are in order. We went many years with a computer without an encyclopedia for it. When I had the opportunity to buy my favorite encyclopedia (*World Book*) on CD-Rom for a decent price, I did it. It was over a year before we even installed it on the computer. And it's been used once since then, when one of my sons had a research project to do that required lots of little pieces of information quickly. It excelled for that purpose, and I imagine that the day might come when I can say that we got our money's worth out of it. But if I had it to do again, I wouldn't spend the money. (In fact, we got 100 years of *National Geographics* on CD's a few years back – and we use those much more often than the *World Book*.)

Computer encyclopedias can certainly serve a useful purpose for some. (Missionary friends were thrilled to be able to take it on the mission field with them – where space and weight were both such critical issues.) And if a home school family has to choose between that or no set of encyclopedias at all, then I would definitely recommend the computer version. {And of course, now most of us are using internet encyclopedias, so much of this section is obsolete – but my family still uses the printed version when we have the opportunity!}

But for those of us with the space, my personal preference is a good set (or two!) of encyclopedias sitting conveniently on the bookshelf. There they are so easy to reference, so easy to curl up with, just inviting someone with a few minutes to sit down and browse (something a computer has never invited me to do!) In fact, when my 14-year-old is in-between G.A. Henty books, he's been known to grab an encyclopedia on his way to bed, for his "light" bedtime reading. He's been overheard in front of the World Books muttering to himself, "Which letter shall I read tonight?" Something he would obviously not be doing with a computer encyclopedia!

Dictionaries

Every family, home schooling or not, should have at least one of these in very easy reach, preferably something good like a *Merriam Webster Collegiate Dictionary*.

Someone in our family probably references the dictionary an average of once a day – to check the pronunciation of a word, the meaning of a word, the origin of a word, and occasionally even the spelling of a word. Dictionaries (and encyclopedias) are often consulted to settle a friendly argument between two family members, or in response to one of Mom's favorite lines, "Look it up".

A point here, on both dictionaries and encyclopedias: we have never felt the need to have a class in dictionary usage or to assign something to be looked up in the encyclopedia, just to practice. Does that mean such efforts are not valid? No, hopefully just not necessary. These tools are an important part of our daily lives, and learning how and when to use them comes naturally as the need arises, in a connected context.

Biblical Reference Tools

When it comes to Biblical references, we use the *Online Bible* on the computer the most often. With it we can compare versions, do words searches and word counts in the Bible, and much more. I also bought a copy of *The Bible Visual Resource Book* about ten years ago. It is absolutely wonderful. It has maps, timelines, book summaries, and so much more. I use it regularly in our "home school" and in our "family worship". We also enjoy our *Strong's Compete Concordance*, *The Topical Bible*, a *Hebrew-English Interlinear Bible*, and a number of good commentaries.

Summary

A home school library should contain a number of good reference books: encyclopedias, dictionaries, a thesaurus, *Shrunk & White*,[47] just to name a few. These can all be bought without straining the budget and are well worth the shelf space they require.

And our home school students should be regular users of our various reference books – knowing where to find the answer is often more critical than actually knowing the answer. Buy the books, use them regularly yourself, and train your children to use them often.

---

[47] *The Elements of Style* by William Strunk Jr. and E.B. White.

"WE FIRMLY BELIEVE LEARNING CAN AND SHOULD BE FUN. WE DO MAKE OUR KIDS DO SOME THINGS THEY DON'T WANT TO, OR THAT THEY DON'T ENJOY -- BUT THAT IS THE EXCEPTION NOT THE RULE. EDUCATION DOES NOT HAVE TO BE BORING, OR ROUTINE. IT SHOULD NOT BE A CHORE."[48]

Fun

It's a shame to think how many people might be surprised to have a chapter on Fun in a home education book!

I had confiscated a water gun from one of my children recently. Instead of dumping the water out like I usually do, I started squirting all the kids that came close to me. (It was amazing how many I got wet before I ran out of water!) When I finished my squirting frenzy, we were all laughing. My 9-year-old looked at me with great surprise afterwards and remarked: "I thought grownups were boring." And recently, when I was discussing a new game we had with my

---

[48] Quote from our *Creative Learning Connection* catalog [when we actually had a catalog! Now we just list things on our website: www.CreativeLearningConnection.com]

8-year-old, she expressed in frustration to me, "Adults don't learn (games) as fast as kids."

I'm not against **having fun**; I just want my children to understand that entertaining themselves should not be their first priority in life. And that wasting time is indeed a terrible waste.

Educational activities can be fun, fun can be educational, and those are my preferences. Why waste time watching an "entertaining" show – when there's something educational and enjoyable on the History Channel? Why play a game that teaches little, when I have shelves full of games that are fun **and** educational? Why play a mindless video game, when we can put together a 1000-piece puzzle?

"I think the man who above all others should be pitied is the man who has never learned how to amuse himself without mechanical assistance when he is alone…an uneducated man, shrinks from quiet. An educated man longs for it"[49]…since he knows he can always read or meditate. Quiet, unscheduled time, for ourselves and our children should be seen as a blessing, not a curse.

My kids are not supposed to use the word "bored"…. After all, being bored is really a choice, a state of mind. To admit to being bored is to admit to making the choice of not doing anything productive. At my house there is no shortage of readily available materials with which to "do something" – games, puzzles, craft materials, etc., so I have little patience

---

[49] *Education, Christianity, and the State*, pg 125-126

with someone who chooses to be bored. My primary solution for a "bored" child is to give him extra chores to occupy his time. That cures the problem very quickly!

There is another side to the "fun issue": Can school be fun? Can learning be fun? Or do we look at fun as something we do after school? How much of what our students need to learn can they be working on through games, songs, or other "creative connections" to the brain?

Is the "fun learning" something we hold over our students' heads – "after you finish your assignment, you can play that game, or put together that puzzle"? Maybe we need to reevaluate what we consider is "real school". My proposition: If learning is taking place – education is in effect. And education counts as 'real school', even if it's outside the scope of a packaged curriculum. If learning is fun, we have less resistance, they want to continue it longer, and they will retain more of it.

Some of our favorite "educational-fun" activities include:

Legos
Toys with small pieces are such a problem in a big family with many small children. We have banned many games and toys over the years just because of the mess and problems that the small pieces pose. But Legos and Duplos fit in a

special category. They have such educational value that we put up with the aggravations they cause. Building with Legos can occupy any number of children (and adults) from ages three and above, for hours at a time. And real thinking goes into many of the models that are built.

On their own initiative, some of my middle sons recently built a model of the ironside, the *U.S.S. Monitor*. They researched their project carefully to make sure they were as accurate as possible. Now mind you, this was not from a kit, it was something they came up with on their own, and spent hours working on. These types of projects strengthen their thinking skills – and they don't even realize they're learning!

Playing Cards
I know that some Christians don't consider cards acceptable. But we don't have a problem with the idea of playing cards in our home.

We would be lost without multiple decks of playing cards around our home. Cards are an inexpensive, portable, versatile activity. The youngest to the oldest can be occupied with them. Younger children can match colors and numbers, even with a partial deck of cards. Memory games are wonderful, and put various ages on an equal footing; my 6-year-old usually beats me in these games. We enjoy various card games with anywhere from one to twelve players. Most of the games we play build thinking skills and the ability to strategize.

Chess

Chess is a wonderful tool to develop thinking skills. It is inexpensive, fairly easy to learn, but difficult to master. It will occupy one or more students for great lengths of time. (At different times in the past we've put together Chess Clubs – which were lots of additional fun!)

Puzzles

Puzzles are great builders of both visual skills and thinking skills. Ravensburger Puzzles have been our all-time favorites, with 24 to 5,000 pieces. Beautiful pictures and quality pieces make them a real joy to put together by all ages. Larger puzzles can be put together as a cooperative effort by many family members.

More about Games

Games can be store-bought or home-made. When you are considering games to purchase, look for games that are

- Educational
- Versatile
- Long Lasting (enjoyable to play for years to come)
- Economical (cheaper is not always the best investment)

Some of the best games in the world are coming out of Germany. I was reading an article in a recent *U.S. News and World Report*[50] that discussed this phenomenon. German

---

[50] December 9, 2002 issue

games topped 7 out of 10 of *Games Magazine*'s 2002 categories. German games are often more expensive – because they are so well built – but they are generally worth the investment. Our current game collection (over 100 games) includes a number of games that we bought when we were in Germany over a dozen years ago. German games tend to include more strategy than their American counterparts, and are generally fast-paced.

Educational games can be considered part of our "curriculum package".[51] Retention is aided when the students are having fun while learning. Games can introduce a concept, or help reinforce an existing lesson. They do not have to be saved until "after school", they can be **part** of school. Buy good games to supplement your other materials – or make your own! Or better yet, have your students make them! What a great way to reinforce learning.

Summary

These are just a "few of our favorite things", and the time they take all qualifies as "school time"! Don't feel like "fun learning" is an oxymoron. The "fun learning" is what kids are more likely to enjoy and remember.

---

[51] I talk more about specific games in the various other chapters.

> "IF MY PEOPLE, WHO ARE CALLED BY
> MY NAME, WILL HUMBLE THEMSELVES AND
> PRAY AND SEEK MY FACE AND TURN FROM
> THEIR WICKED WAYS, THEN WILL I HEAR
> FROM HEAVEN AND WILL FORGIVE
> THEIR SIN AND WILL HEAL THEIR LAND."
> 2 CHRONICLES 7:14

Geography

Geography is not really a separate subject to teach, it should be incorporated into History, Bible, Literature…Teach it in context!

What are the primary goals in teaching our students geography?
- How it impacts on the lives of people.
- What are the secondary goals in teaching our students geography?

Recognition of:
- Continents (and countries and states…)
- Oceans
- Major rivers

- Longitude and Latitude (Tropics of Cancer, Capricorn, Equator)
- Most of these come up naturally as you are teaching other areas "in context". Look for them, and grasp the opportunity. My students have won geography bees, but they've never taken a "geography class".

Good geography resources:
- World map/globe
- Map puzzles
- Road Maps and Atlases (especially on trips) From a very young age my oldest son learned to navigate for the family on our trips, a skill that serves him well as he travels across the country and the world.
- Games (*Risk, Journey Through Europe, Geodyssey 10 Days in Asia, 10 Days in the Americas...*)

Final Thoughts on Geography
Maps should be a part of any home school "curriculum". Many used book stores sell old *National Geographic* maps for a very inexpensive price, and there are many good books and programs that include blank maps you can copy to use with your history and Bible programs. Please be sure to use maps often, in your home "school" and in your home life.

"TO US IN PARTICULAR WHO ARE LIVING IN ONE OF THE GREAT EPOCHS OF HISTORY IT IS NECESSARY TO KNOW SOMETHING OF WHAT HAS GONE BEFORE IN ORDER TO THINK JUSTLY OF WHAT IS OCCURRING TODAY."
CHARLOTTE MASON

History

Don't teach in a vacuum – connection is critical to learning! "Historical events are interesting to us mainly in connection with feelings, the sufferings, and interests of those by whom they are accomplished. In history, we are surrounded by men long dead, but whose deeds survive..."[52]

In other words, history is about people. That's what makes it interesting, that's what makes it important. We are seeing God's work in the lives of people through the ages, when we study history. Dates are only hooks on which to hang information – let's put our emphasis on the information, not the hooks.

I didn't begin life as a "history buff" -- Throughout high school I memorized the material, aced the tests, and then did a "memory dump". Here's what made it change for me:

---

[52] *A Charlotte Mason Companion*, pg 32

- Being in the midst of history
- Seeing it
- Touching it
- Putting it in perspective
- Making the connections

I was so excited about the history around us when we lived in Germany that I wrote my first book![53] That's what our children need – excitement. When we're excited, it rubs off on our children. One of the greatest novels written about the Civil War is *Killer Angels*, about the battle of Gettysburg. Author Michael Shaara, did such a great job sharing his excitement for history, that his son, Jeff, has gone on to write at least four other wonderful historical novels.

My 11-year-old and 13-year-old sons recently attended a History Day Camp. On the last day, I was having a conversation with the Camp Instructor. He said almost apologetically to me, "Well, I hope I was able to teach your sons some history this past week. They already knew so much when they started." I share that with you not to brag, but to show you how our excitement for a subject can rub off on our children. And yes, they did learn at the History Camp. Who can ever run out of things to learn?

---

[53] *An American Looks At Wuerzburg* – Finally reprinted in 2009!

But are we teaching history the way **we** "learned" it? Remember, covering material is not the same as learning it!!! We forget sometimes that we need to do more than just "cover subjects" and check them off the list. We don't just want to **teach** a subject, we want our students to **learn** it as well.

There are two main ways to teach anything:
1. Expose the students to it. (That's what textbooks usually do…again and again and again…This qualifies as "covering" a subject; but not necessarily learning it)

2. Immerse the students in it (real learning can take place this way). Obviously, I prefer immersion. We have to get their attention. We have to make it interesting. We have to repeat the process, we have to reinforce the facts.

History is everywhere. Find it. See it. Touch it. Relate to it. Start with something they can see/touch:
- Museums
- Battlefields
- Historic Homes
- Cemeteries

These will all make history "come alive" for our students!

Experiencing History along the Lewis & Clark Trail

Compare that to most standard curriculums: Textbooks are typically boring! One reason is that they don't go deep enough into any particular person or event. Another reason is that they're two-dimensional (just the pages in a book), not three-dimensional (real people, experiences, etc.), and there is little variety in teaching methods. How are we going to get and hold our students' attention that way?

One of the big concerns in putting aside the textbooks is that we might "miss something". There might be gaps in their learning. How will we know what to study when? In the *Multi-level Teaching* chapter, I have a chart showing the history scope and sequences from three different major Christian publishing companies. They are all different. They vary greatly. And they prove quite well that there is not "one way" to teach history, one "correct order" that must be followed. So why not consider something else?

- Why not biographies? (like *Childhood of Famous Americans* and *Trailblazers*)
- Historical fiction? (The Shaara books; books by Bodie Thoene…)
- Movies? (*The Hiding Place; Gettysburg; October Sky...*)
- Games? (*Chronology; Civil War Time-line Game*)
- Audios? (*Odyssey, Your Story Hour, Principles of American History*)

Connect it to something they like:
- Math: *Mathematicians are People, Too* by Luetta and Wilbert Reimer
- Art: *Winston Churchill, His Life as a Painter* by his daughter, Mary Soames
- Astronomy: The history of astronomy

Or start with something that is relevant to them now:
- An election (A great time to start a study of the Presidents)
- Where they live (We studied the Middle Ages in Germany, the Civil War in Alabama.)
- A holiday (Why not start a study of the Pilgrims in November?)

A chronological approach works, but it's not necessary. (See above!)

- Timelines work well to see things in order.
- Personal timeline books are a great way to organize what each student is studying.
- Make your own.
- Or buy one that someone else developed.

What's important in a timeline book?
- Space to write dates
- Space to draw pictures
- Space for notes
- More space in recent years, since we typically have more information there.

Historical Games reinforce what they're learning.
- Purchase one or more:

- *Chronology, Time-line Games*[54] – World History, Civil War, Presidents...
    - *Risky Strategy* & *Hail to the Chief* (election-related board games)

- Make your own:
    - Family History
    - To go with a topic you've been studying

Great history books:
- *The American Adventures* series (U.S. History)
- Books by G.A. Henty (World History, very little U.S. History)
- Bodie Thoene's *Zion Covenant and Zion Chronicles* (WWII and Israel)

Great Additional History Resources
- Dover Coloring Books[55] (wonderful way to reinforce history)
- *National Geographic* (often slightly edited, to remove pictures, etc.)

For ideas on topics to start with if you want to break away from history textbooks, please see the *Unit Study* chapter.

Final Thoughts on History
We heard recently[56] that college graduates today know less about history than high school graduates did 50 years ago. May home schoolers help to reverse that trend!

---

[54] We have made numerous time-line games, on everything from the Revolutionary War to Presidents to the History of Astronomy.
[55] More on Dover Coloring Books in the *Indispensable* chapter.
[56] Paul Harvey radio show, December 2002

"ARE THESE THINGS THEN NECESSITIES? THEN LET US MEET THEM LIKE NECESSITIES."
~KING HENRY IN SHAKESPEARE'S HENRY IV, PART 2

Indispensable homeschooling books, sites, etc...

Necessary or Unnecessary Items?

It helps to know what you really need, and what you can live without, especially if you're homeschooling on a tight budget. Here are my guidelines for what I really, *really* find important, and what I consider less critical. Look them over, but please, make your own list!

Very Important	Fairly Important	Not So Important
Paper – white (lots!)	Heavy Duty 3-Hole Punch	School Desks
Books	Books – lots of them!	Computers
3-ring Binders	Globe	Textbooks
Maps	Wall Maps – World/U.S.	Teacher's Guides
3-hole Punch	Page Protectors	
Dictionary	Educational Games	
Encyclopedia set[57]	Paper Cutter	
(not a very long list, is it?)	White Out Pens	
	Paper – colors	

---

[57] I had actually started with this in the middle column, until my daughter and I discussed again how much we used our set.

My Favorite Home Education Websites
{These are new, but they have been added not so much because they didn't fit in the "Americanized" Organized Ramblings, but because I didn't know about them when I did the second edition of that.}

www.CurrClick.com

A website where thousands of great educational materials can be bought as e-books and downloaded anywhere in the world. Many are even free!

http://www.homeschoolfreebie.wholesomechildhood.com/

A website where you can sign up to get weekly emails that tell you about the upcoming daily freebies. Oftentimes some great resources that cost you nothing but your time and effort!

My Favorite (Home) Education Authors
- Ruth Beechick
- John Taylor Gatto
- John Holt
- Mary Hood
- Dr. Raymond and Dorothy Moore

My Favorite (Home) Education Books
- *You can Teach Your Child Successfully* by Ruth Beechick
- *The Joyful Homeschooler* by Mary Hood
- *The Simplicity of Homeschooling by* Vicki Goodchild
- *Dumbing Us Down* by John Taylor Gatto

Ruth Beechick's book has ideas for teaching grades 4 – 8 and beyond! The BEST home schooling book I have ever read. Ruth tells you about teaching everything from READING to WRITING to HISTORY to MUSIC. If you are just getting started, or need a boost, this is the book to give you encouragement! Ruth also has three smaller books with information on teaching K-3rd grade: Reading, Language, and Arithmetic; also excellent books.

1	2	3	4	5	6	7	8	9	10
11	12	13	14	15	16	17	18	19	20
21	22	23	24	25	26	27	28	29	30
31	32	33	34	35	36	37	38	39	40
41	42	43	44	45	46	47	48	49	50
51	52	53	54	55	56	57	58	59	60
61	62	63	64	65	66	67	68	69	70
71	72	73	74	75	76	77	78	79	80
81	82	83	84	85	86	87	88	89	90
91	92	93	94	95	96	97	98	99	100

Ruth was the first to show me the great versatility and usefulness of the Hundred's Chart!

My Favorite Magazine {also available on-line}
Ideas on Liberty from the Foundation for Economic Education – a monthly magazine that deals with economic issues from a conservative perspective.

    Foundation for Economic Education
    30 Broadway
    Irvington-on-Hudson, NY 10533
    (800) 960-4333
    www.fee.org

Other Favorites
We use *The Book of Psalms for Singing*[58] and *the Book of Psalms Translated for Singing*,[59] and *Psalm Settings*[60] in our family worship times.

---

[58] This one is complete, with music, and several songs for some of the psalms.

Psalm Singing Books
> Crown & Covenant Publications
> 7408 Penn Ave.
> Pittsburg, PA 15208-2531
> (412) 241-0436
> http://www.psalms4u.com/

Summary
There are very few things you *have* to have in order to teach your children at home. If you prayerfully consider what items are truly indispensable in *your* home schooling venture it will save your family time, money and stress!

[And as we've moved further into the 21st century, more and more educational resources are available on-line – making homeschooling even easier when money and/or space is tight.] {And when shipping options are limited or expensive...}

---

[59] This book only has one song for each psalm, and doesn't have the music, it merely lists a tune that works.

[60] *Psalm Settings* just gives a few psalms set to familiar tunes.

> "BUT THOSE WHO WAIT ON THE LORD SHALL RENEW THEIR STRENGTH; THEY SHALL MOUNT UP WITH WINGS LIKE EAGLES, THEY SHALL RUN AND NOT BE WEARY, THEY SHALL WALK AND NOT FAINT." ~ISAIAH 40:31

Jumping Jacks & Fitness

PE (Physical Education) is another aspect of our home schooling experience that intimidates many. There are many options to fulfill this particular "subject". It need not be another burden we face, another of the myriad subjects we must "work" into our overflowing schedules.

One month I kept an Exercise Log for the members of our family. That month's physical activities included:

- Horseback Riding
- Walking
- Football
- Volleyball
- Weights & Exercises
- Ballroom Dancing
- Jump Roping
- Bike Riding
- Kickball

My students' exercise times that month ranged from 3½ hours to 20 hours.

PE options include:
- Personal exercise & Individual sports
    - Walking
    - Roller Blading/Skating
    - Ice Skating
    - Weights & Exercises
- Organized PE classes
    - At someone's home
    - At a local gym
- Swimming
    - Lessons/Swim Teams
    - Lap Swimming
- Team sports
    - Soccer
    - Lacrosse
    - Baseball

Our family takes care of some of our PE needs with a weekly Boys' PE time for boys 11 and up in our front yard. My 16-year-old son runs the program. An average of a dozen boys come weekly to play football, baseball, ultimate frisbee, scramble and more. All it required to set this up was some space, some word of mouth advertising to homeschoolers in and out of our support group, and a little PE equipment that we already owned. I make sure I'm home when it's scheduled, but other than that I personally have to do very little for it. A similar program could be done for girls just as easily, I don't currently have girls that age. As my younger girls get older, I'll have to consider expanding our program![61]

My family has also participated in organized sports on many occasions in the last seventeen years, and will undoubtedly do so again. Our children have participated in ballet, tap, gymnastics and fencing; and played on soccer, baseball, football, rugby [and lacrosse] teams. Overall, those seasons have been positive experiences. My biggest complaint about them is the time commitment they require. If your family is considering such an activity for the first time, especially the sports, be sure you count the costs in time commitment. I often wonder if I'll keep my sanity when we're in the middle of a sports season, and am quite relieved when it ends. (And then we turn around and do it again the next season!) In other words, "beware the organized sports trap" – understand what it will do to your schedule, before you commit.

---

[61] Though I will add, I don't think a PE class just for girls is as critical as it is for boys. Not that girls need exercise less than boys – but I don't think they need the *group* experience like guys do. (I go into that more at the end of the *Teaching Teens* chapter.)

One of the sports experiences we have enjoyed much more are the soccer programs that two of our support groups have organized over the years. They only met once a week instead of multiple times, and the various ages all met in one location. Fun/exercise/learning a sport – all rolled into one.

Another beneficial PE activity is the President's Physical Fitness program. It is an easy thing for even a small home school group to organize, and gives the kids something to train for during the year. One way we've done this is to have a President's Physical Fitness day in the fall, so everyone can see the standards, and get motivated. And then we had another one in the spring, after many of them had trained hard to improve their personal scores. (More information on the program and the events can be found at: www.indiana.edu/~preschal/index.shtml)

In Conclusion
We want our children to be physically active without it becoming another drain on the schedule and the budget. As you can see, PE can take many forms. Work it into your family's schedule and preferences. May our children be able to say in both a physical and spiritual sense, "God is my strength and power: and He maketh my way perfect."[62]

---

[62] 2 Samuel 22:33

"THE CAT WILL MEW,
AND THE DOG WILL HAVE HIS DAY."
HAMLET IN SHAKESPEARE'S HAMLET

Kids (the 4 legged kind)

I do not consider myself an "animal person". For many years I could conveniently shrug off the possibility of having pets – we were moving too often, and we had too little space. Besides, my time was being well occupied with my own "two-legged kids".

But alas, all that changed. In 1997 we moved to a new home – complete with four acres, a dog pen, a barn, a back pasture, and a creek on the edge of the property. Suddenly all my good excuses for not having animals were evaporating. We started slowly – my husband only wanted two Labrador Retrievers "to protect our children from the creek" – which they have actually done: one of our labs helped save our then 3-year-old son Elijah from drowning.

My life was only mildly interrupted by the addition of two dogs – daily feedings/house training/ monthly medicine/yearly checkups and rabies shots/and the occasional "extra" trip to the vet. Not <u>too</u> overwhelming. And other than the driving, our children were doing all the work with the dogs.

That was the first year. Then one of my older sons decided we should get goats – for the milk. Fencing became an issue (a big issue, in fact). We added milking and feeding goats to the daily routine. And then there were the four horses we added the following year...At one point we had more animals than children, which took some doing! Five years after getting "into" animals we're now back to just the two dogs we started with. (Well, at least we were when I *started* this chapter – we just adopted another dog, and may be taking in a fourth. So much for downsizing.)

The positive aspects of our experiences with animals are many: My children learned much from the daily exercise of caring for the family herd, and the goat's milk was a nice addition to the family diet. The children are fairly good at riding horses now. They have become more comfortable around horses than I am. (Those were some BIG animals! I helped feed them for less than a week, and I was intimidated.)

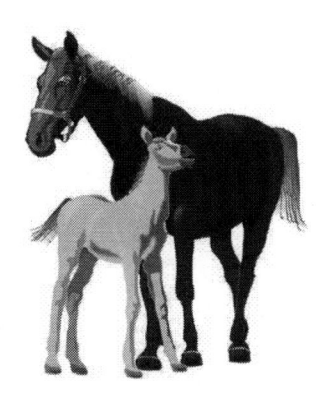

Seven of them have now milked goats. (I haven't!) The kids (the 2-legged kind) also learned about life (mating and birth) and death, responsibility, budgeting, and more. Animals were, and still are, an important part of our regular "schoolwork".

There were also some negatives to having so many animals: The total costs always seemed to be higher than we had budgeted; family trips suddenly became much more complicated, and *every* day had to start and end with thinking of the animal chores.

Final Thoughts
I tell you all this to share with you a little of what I have learned – go into animals slowly and carefully; it's easier to get in than to get out. Have a good idea how much you can afford to spend (and plan as if the costs will be higher than you had expected, because they probably will). Don't forget to expect the unexpected, the vet bills for accidents/illness/etc. Talk to others who have been there

first. But also remember, you won't really know what it's like until you've done it. And it can be very good for your children in so many ways. If you try it for a while, you can always stop again if your family doesn't like it.

Of course, if you get to that point, that will be another part of the experience – parting with animals that have become "a part of the family". Selling or giving away animals that we've had has always been easier emotionally for me than for my children! Actually, that's not quite true – our two labs have been with us for over 5 years – and any attempt to get rid of them now generally meets with the greatest resistance from *me*. [When our second lab died in 2009, I was one of the ones to grieve the most....she had been with our family longer than our youngest child at that point...So it is a bittersweet feeling to be animal-free for the first time in more than 12 years.]

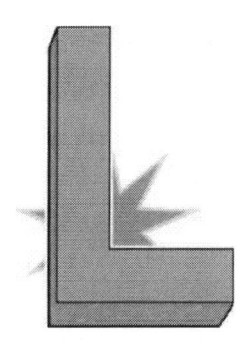

> "BUT WHEN JESUS SAW IT, HE WAS GREATLY DISPLEASED AND SAID TO THEM, "LET THE LITTLE CHILDREN COME TO ME... FOR SUCH IS THE KINGDOM OF GOD."
> MARK 10:14

The "Littles" of the Family

Where do our "littles" fit into the picture as we educate our older children? We have currently been home educating for over 20 years, and until a couple of years ago, we always had at least three that were under school age.

One of the beauties of using as few textbooks as we do is that it is easier to manage the "littles" during school time. Younger children are often interested in listening to the books we read aloud and to the discussions we frequently have. When they are interested in what we're doing, they hang around. When they're not, they typically go off and play with legos. Since I spend so little time making lesson plans or checking assignments or grading tests, there is really very little time when I even think of my pre-schoolers as "being in the way" during school time. So, occupying them during that time is not such a tough issue for us as it is for some families.

Additionally the number of small children I've always had works *for* me, not *against* me; there are always at least two "nonschoolers" who can keep each other company when the "olders" are engaged in school work. I must admit to another "secret" here — that I'll go into more in the *Others* chapter. When I conduct formal classes for older students, a friend watches my younger kids in exchange for her older kids being in the class. We all benefit that way.

We do not use a formal pre-school or kindergarten program (surprise!) in our home. We subscribe pretty much to the Moore's *Better Late Than Early* philosophy. But our younger children get plenty of informal education all the same. Young children need time, experiences, and guided fun, *not* "schoolwork". They also need repetition, repetition, repetition. (That's why they want the same story read over and over again, even if we would rather not.)

Counting
Counting is something that comes naturally, as does adding and subtracting. (Cookies and candy work well for those skills! If you don't eat those things in your family, I'm sure you can find a suitable substitute.) We work on letters of the alphabet and numbers as we go about our day-to-day life. My 4-year-old is quite versed in all those "subjects" — without ever having taken a "class".

Manipulatives
We use many manipulatives in our "preschool":
- Pattern Blocks

- Cuisenaire Rods
- Interlocking Cubes
- Puzzles
- Geoboards
- Play Dough
- Legos
- Dominoes

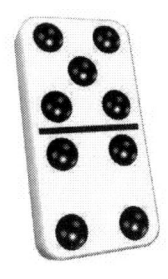

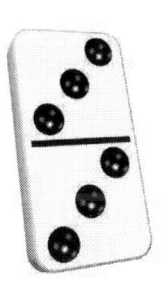

These are all great fun – and wonderfully educational.

Games

Many games teach number, color, and shape recognition. They also can teach counting, patience (taking turns), and thinking skills (strategy). We especially like playing card games and memory games with this age.

Alphabet

My oldest ones have an alphabet book we put together when they were younger. It has a page for each letter, and something about the related field trip we did for that letter. For instance, "A" shows them in front of an airplane and says, "They went to the Airport, and that was A". "J" shows them jumping on a trampoline with their cousin Jill. It wasn't a lot of work to do, it was fun, and even after all these years, it's special to them.

Letters make a nice "hook". We've done a "letter a week" many times over the years – where we did as much each week as we could with that week's letter: books, songs, food, activities, all started with that week's letter.

Summary

Children learn so much from what's going on around them, when we don't even realize it. We were on our way to see my 11-year-old, Immanuel, in one of his fencing classes. As we were going in, my 3-year-old, Sonia, realized she did not know what fencing was, and she asked, "What is fencing?" Since our older kids had been studying Hamlet, and I knew she had seen at least portions of the videos, I compared it to that: "It's like the sword fighting in Hamlet." To which she quickly responded: "And then will Manny say, 'I die Horatio, I die.'?" Don't underestimate what your "littles" are learning, even without a lot of work on your part!

"IT NEVER SEEMS TO OCCUR TO MANY MODERN TEACHERS THAT THE PRIMARY BUSINESS OF THE TEACHER IS TO STUDY THE SUBJECT THAT HE IS GOING TO TEACH."[63]

Multi-level Teaching

Even if you only have one student, please don't skip this chapter! There will be plenty that is still applicable to your family!

Many folks wrongly pity those of us with large families, thinking remorsefully of the extra work we must face, and of how hard it must be for us to meet the needs of so many, especially when they find out we're educating our children at home. And there are families with multiple children who really do work much harder when it comes to the education of their children. But for those of us who practice "multi-level" teaching, the chore is really not that much more difficult than for those who teach only one. (In fact, as I'll explain later, in many cases, it is an *easier* task for us!)

---

[63] *Education, Christianity, & The State* – pg 14
(Which is one of the reasons I like multi-level teaching so much – its efficiency.)

First, though, a definition: "multi-level" teaching is simply taking two or more students who are not at the same level, but teaching them the same subject at the same time anyway. That is the secret to teaching and enjoying students who are at vastly different places in their education.

Second, in preparing this chapter, I realized that there are at least two things I dislike even more than Textbooks: <u>Grade Levels</u> and <u>Scope & Sequences</u>.

Being in bondage to those two things keeps us from doing effective multi-level teaching. And it keeps us bound to the textbooks that go with them.

Let me explain the term, "scope and sequence": A scope and sequence spells out what will be covered for a subject each year (scope) and in what order (sequence). Every textbook publishing company I've looked at has one.

But let me point out several things about any particular scope and sequence:
- It shows what is covered each year, not what is learned.
- It is an artificial starting and ending point.
- It splits up a family's education process, rather than uniting it.
- It is man-made, not divinely inspired.

(Even among Christian companies, there are vast differences, see the chart on the next page)

- It is usually very shallow by definition, since it covers so much, and thus cannot get very deep.

Does that mean that a particular scope and sequence and the textbook that accompanies it is worthless? No, we can use it as a tool. Use it to get ideas from. But don't feel tied to it. Your family's scope and sequence will be different than mine. Under God's direction, let the interests, desires, strengths, and weaknesses of your family dictate your academic schedules.

I made the following chart to show the differences in scope and sequences between several Christian publishing companies.

	A Beka	BJU	Alpha Omega
1st	Good Citizenship	U.S. pre-Columbus → 1600's	Community
2nd	"Our America'	U.S. Jamestown → Revolution	Community
3rd	Biographies of Famous Americans	U.S. Constitution → Civil War and Westward Expansion	U.S. Geography (certain areas)
4th	U.S.	U.S. late 1700's → early 1900's	Regions - Island/Mtn/Polar/...
5th	Old World (w/geography)	U.S. early 1900's → Present	U.S. History w/ U.S. Geography
6th	New World (w/geography)	Ancient World (→ Middle Ages)	World History
7th	World	World (beyond Dark Ages)	Anthropology, Sociology, Economics, Political Science...
8th	U.S.	U.S.	U.S.
9th	Government & Economics	Geography	Government
10th	World (w/Culture)	World	World
11th	U.S.	U.S.	U.S.
12th	Economics	Economics/Government	Political...

Still think there's just one right order to teach history?

Which of these scope & sequences is right? Why is one better than another? Or better than your own? Who says 8th & 11th graders have to study U.S. history? Why can't you teach that to your 8th & 9th graders together? Or your 10th and 12th graders?

Grade levels are all so artificial. What does being a "3rd grader" really mean? Or a 6th grader? Or an 8th? Our family only "worries" about grade levels for social reasons (Scouts, Awanas, Sunday schools and grandparents!) Until graduation time, what difference does it really make anyway?

As an aside, if you ever want to depress yourself, take a look at the various graded curriculum guides in the series with *What Your 4th Grader Should Know*. (I actually enjoyed the first Cultural Literacy book E.D. Hirsch, Jr. wrote, *Cultural Literacy: What Every American Needs to Know*. But his grade level guides, which pinpoint at what grade such literacy should be acquired, are very intimidating and unrealistic.)

So the first key to multi-level teaching is to understand that grade levels and scope and sequences are artificial, and that they don't need to dictate what <u>your</u> family studies, or <u>when</u>.

Now we can get down to the nitty gritty of multi-level teaching:
- <u>How</u> do I do this?
- <u>What</u> can I teach this way?

Well, second question first…Almost anything. Teaching a child to read would be one exception, and much of math would be another exception. But just about anything else can be taught this way:

Bible

I firmly believe that Bible should be taught as a multi-level subject. What possible gain can come from having your children each do totally different assignments in Bible? None. And the loss is very great. We want them to reinforce each other's learning in Bible! When they study it *together*, meaningful discussion can increase, and so can retention.

Writing

So much of writing ought to be copywork. Copywork is simply copying passages that someone else has written – from the Bible, classical literature, Shakespeare quotes, etc. George Washington practiced copywork as a young man, and Charlotte Mason recommended it for educators over 100 years ago. Ruth Beechick touches on it in her book *You Can Teach Your Child Successfully* and Cindy Rushton explains it in great detail in *Language Arts the Easy Way*. As copywork, writing can easily be a multi-level subject. You just assign longer passages to the older ones and have higher expectations for the quality of their handwriting.[64]

Math

Math is the only subject that we do on a more individual basis, because of the way it builds. But even there, much of it

---

[64] This doesn't make copywork simply a handwriting exercise. By copying quality writing, students improve their own writing styles and they learn better grammar.

can be done together as a family (sharing specific concepts such as fractions[65]; measurements; time; money...what is grade specific about any of those?)

And there are wonderful books like *Mathematicians are People, Too!* that can be read aloud to multiple ages. These books are small biographical sketches of mathematicians and are a great introduction to different people and different mathematical concepts.

History and Science
History and Science beg to be taught as multi-level subjects. I can't imagine not doing them that way anymore. These are covered more in-depth in the *History and Geography* chapter and the *Nature and Other Sciences* chapter. Please look at those for more information.

---

[65] Measuring cups convey fractions easily and well!

But then comes the How question:
You need a starting point – a textbook, a unit study, or a particular topic of interest.

Yes, *this* is when a textbook can be useful. Pick one for science and one for history, for example – *not* a different one for each grade.
- Start with the textbook if you would like. "Do it" together. Read it aloud. Discuss it.
- Dig deeper. (Get out those encyclopedias.)
- Read "real books" (books that were meant to be read & enjoyed) that go with it.
- Read aloud times/Silent reading

Copywork can be done with this.
- Discuss what you've studied (You don't have to do the tests & questions.)
- There are all sorts of other ways to document – pictures/copywork/maps...
- Assignments can include:
    - Interviews
    - Plays
    - Related Puzzles
    - Games
    - Remember – you are in control!
    - Teach your *students*, not the textbooks.

When you are working with several students on the same topic, your life will be easier and they will reinforce each other's learning. Remember, learning comes with repetition, and this way, you're not the only one being repetitive!

For the ultimate way to incorporate multi-level teaching into your schooling, please take a look at the *Unit Studies* chapter.

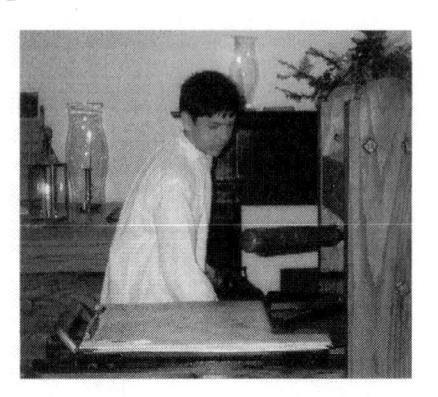

Conclusion

You know your family better than textbook developers. You have their best interests in mind, that's why you're teaching them at home. Only you can decide what they need when – not me, not your best friend, and certainly not the big curriculum providers! For the sake of your family, please prayerfully and carefully consider these thoughts.

"WHAT IS THE WORK OF CREATION? THE WORK OF CREATION IS, GOD'S MAKING ALL THINGS OF NOTHING, BY THE WORD OF HIS POWER, IN THE SPACE OF SIX DAYS, AND ALL VERY GOOD."[66]

Nature and Other Sciences

I consider myself to be more an historian than a scientist. And our home school schedule definitely reflects that bent. But, we do need to give our children a good taste for the sciences, so I strive to keep some sort of balance.

Science is, after all, the study of God's world and as such is a wonderful subject. So much to see, so much to learn. So exciting. And yet, like history, how many students have learned to detest this subject? How many of them are bored and frustrated with science?

Nature, specifically, is a window to the world God has created. Do we share that wonder with our children? Do we slow down enough to really appreciate nature and to let our children appreciate it? That is another idea I garnered from my study of Charlotte Mason.

Nature is really all the science our younger children need. Walks where they can see and appreciate God's creation. Time to stop and look at the flowers. To study the birds. To

---
[66] Question and Answer 9 from the *Westminster Shorter Catechism*

wonder at the stars. Trips to the park and the zoo, and to our own backyard. (Nature studies were the primary form of education Leonardo da Vinci received in his own childhood 500 years ago[67] – so this isn't a new concept!)

Creation Science Studies

If a family is looking for an elementary science program to use, especially with multiple ages, *Considering God's Creation* is the one I strongly recommend. It is inexpensive, it is adaptable to multiple ages, it is fun, and it is good. What more can I say?

One way or another, our students need a good grounding in Creation Science. If there should be a "required course" for Christian home educators, this would be it!

However we do it, may our children be able to say with Johann Kepler: "I thank Thee, my Creator and Lord, that Thou hast given me this joy in Thy creation, this delight in the works of Thy hands…"[68] and with the psalmist: "When I consider thy heavens, the work of thy fingers, the moon and the starts, which thou has ordained; The heavens declare the glory of God; and the firmament sheweth his handwork."[69]

In addition to Vision Forum's Jonathan Park CDs, our favorite Creation resources are from Answers in Genesis (www.answersingenesis.org) and Institute for Creation Research (www.icr.org).

Science Textbooks

So many homeschoolers depend on textbooks to teach Science that I made the following chart to show the many

---

[67] And he went on to become an incredible scientist, artist, inventor, and much more…
[68] *America's God and Country Encyclopedia of Quotations*, pg 350
[69] Psalm 8:3; 19:1

options in major Science curriculums. Note the significant differences in the first 9 years. Who's right? Who's wrong? Who cares? Sorry, that was to see if you were paying attention! You *should* care. You should care that there is obviously not one right way to teach your family science. There is not a God-given order to these scope and sequences, or some sacredness to the orders picked. Your way will be the best for your family!

Grade	A Beka	BJU	Alpha Omega
1st	Plants, Animals, Energy, Seasons, Senses…	Creation, Animals, Senses, Stars, Sound…	Senses, Animals, Plants, Health, Energy, Machines
2nd	Human Body, Animals, Plants, Energy, Earth/Space	Bones, Plants, Earth (Shape, movement, forces,…)	Plants, Animals, Human Body, Pets, Senses
3rd	Plants, Animals, Weather, Ocean, Desert, Pond…	Animals, Solar System, Skin, Photosynthesis, Birds, Mass & Weights	Human Body, Plants, Animals, Matter, Seasons, Rocks, Energy
4th	Insects, Plants, Birds, Weather, Stars, Ecology	Moon, Light, Electricity, Machines, Digestion, Animals, Trees, Insects	Plants, Animals, Machines, Electricity & Magnetism, Weather, Solar
5th	Scientists & Naturalists (Creationists), Plants, Animals, Matter, Energy, Light, Minerals	Flight, Energy, Weather, Plant &Animal Reproduction, Oceans, Winds, Animals…	Cells, Plants, Animals, Balance in Nature, Energy, Fossils, Geology, Nature Cycles
6th	Creation Vs. Evolution, Animals, Plants, Universe, Space Travels	Earthquakes, Volcanoes, Stars, Chemistry, Blood Circulation, Space…	Plants, Animals, Chemistry, Light & Sound, Solar System, Motion
7th	Soil Science, Plants, Human Body, Weather, Creation, Insects	Life Science	Earth, Atmosphere, Weather, Human Anatomy, Careers
8th	Astronomy, Physics, Magnetism & Electricity, Science vs. Evolution	Earth Science	Health/Nutrition, Energy, Machines, Technology, Balance in Nature
9th	Atmosphere, Weather, Earthquakes, Volcanoes, Rocks, Fossils	"Basic" Science	Geology, Health, Astronomy, Oceanography, Applications
10th	Biology	Biology	Biology
11th	Chemistry	Chemistry	Chemistry
12th	Physics	Physics	Physics

While there is a complete lack of similarity between the three publishers at the younger grades, there is complete agreement between them as to what our $10^{th} - 12^{th}$ graders should study. Does that make it necessarily so? No! What about Geology, Creation Science, Astronomy? The high school science possibilities are almost endless. Please don't fall into the trap that every high schooler has to take biology, chemistry, and physics. Some will, but even those who are college bound do not always *have* to!

Expanding on Science Textbooks
There are other ways to teach Science than those just shown. I talk more about this in the *Multi-level Teaching* chapter and the *Unit Studies* chapter. If you didn't want to start from scratch, you could take your fourth grade science textbook (for example) – if you have one, and pick nine of the many topics from it. Cover one each month, you will cover less of the book, but cover it in-depth. Example:

- Elephants
- Trees
- Butterflies
- Etc.

Or look over the book, pick the first half of the subjects in the table of contents, or the half your family would enjoy the most, and spend twice as long on each topic! Who says a textbook has to be covered in one year anyway?

History of Astronomy

Of course, as a historian I find an historical approach to science is a great way to look at it. Friends of mind did a major "History of Science" class for high schoolers a few years back. I didn't want to tackle all of science, but I thought "History of Astronomy" would be doable and enjoyable. I actually prepared and taught that class to two different age groups (5-7 and 8-12) for one semester, and to junior high/high schoolers for two semesters. We studied a different astronomer each week – looking at their lives and their contributions to astronomy. Coming up with the first list of 10 major astronomers wasn't too difficult, but the second 10 was more challenging. It was a great way to bridge science and history. And almost any subject (in or out of science) can be looked at in this manner!

We don't always have a big official science study going on in our home, but we look for everyday opportunities to study science. Or it might be better to say opportunities find us. A few examples:

Ticks

One night I was holding my three-year-old, Sonia, and discovered that she had a tick on her head. After removing the little critter, we put it in a clear jar with a lid. Six-year-old Elijah quickly announced that the tick had eight legs. I started to comment on it being an insect, and then said, wait a minute, don't insects have six legs?! A quick search of the encyclopedias followed. We finally discovered that ticks are in the same family as spiders, and are not insects, they are in the arachnid family. (It took us three encyclopedias to figure that out.) But now, the two adults, one teenager, and four younger kids who were present at the time are not likely to forget that ticks are not insects. And we didn't need a textbook or a test to accomplish that.

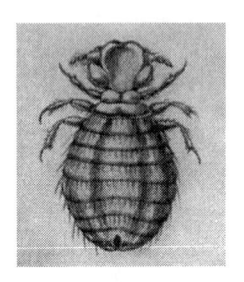

Snails

Friends of ours have lots of snails on their property. They had done a little "unit study" on snails. So Dad brought home a bottle full of 40 or 50 snails from their house for our kids to observe for a while. They did research with their dad on-line and in the encyclopedia about snails (sizes, poisonous vs. non-poisonous, etc.) They even found an easy way to draw snails and tried their hand at that. They put out some bait in our garden to check on our population – they only caught one. It was a brief but fascinating "snail study".

Wasps

My kids caught a wasp-like of insect one evening. Their older sister (our 25-year-old) was babysitting for them, and they were debating amongst themselves as to whether it was a wasp or a hornet. They went on-line, and spent 40 minutes searching for a picture of their catch. They finally did determine that it was a wasp, exactly what type of wasp it was, and that it is a helpful creature to have around, not a harmful one. And neither Mom nor Dad were even home at the time!

Birds

I've been fascinated by birds for some time now. Many years ago we studied birds in a KONOS unit, and we've touched on them now and again, but it's been a long time since I've really studied birds at all with my children. Since moving to Alabama five years ago, we've lived in two different homes, both frequented by many birds. I love waking up to the sounds of birds every morning; and for several years now I've wanted us to study the birds that we see around us. But alas, that's a study that is still being contemplated.

But, because I keep thinking we're going to start it someday, I do pay attention to the birds that fly around our yard. We have the typical birds – robins, blue jays, and cardinals regularly. And even an occasional hummingbird. But recently we were watching some birds in the back yard, and there was a new one I didn't remember seeing before. I called all those who were nearby over to the window to see this unusual bird with the red head that was climbing around on the tree. My 6-year-old, Elijah, came over, looked at it, and quickly announced that we were looking at a woodpecker. When I tried to find the bird in the encyclopedia later, I discovered that Elijah was indeed correct, it had been a woodpecker. When I questioned him as to how he knew it was a woodpecker, he very matter-of-factly said, "Well, Mom, it had a red head, and a woodpecker type of beak." (Please don't laugh at my ignorance of such a basic identification; I really didn't know it was a woodpecker! Just appreciate with me that my son did, even if I didn't!)

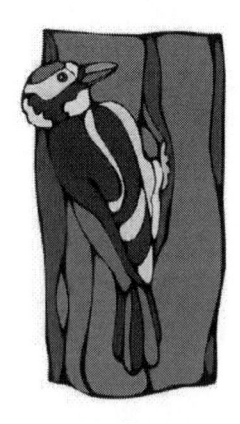

So science clearly doesn't have to come from a textbook, or any book for that matter!

Summary

I don't believe science will ever rise to the level of history in our home – but that hasn't stopped many of my children from enjoying science along the way. In fact, a friend of mine has been giving various hand-on science classes this year and she has commented to me about how well my various students have done in her classes, and how well they grasp scientific principles. Not too bad, considering that at this point, none of those students (the younger seven) have ever worked from a science textbook!

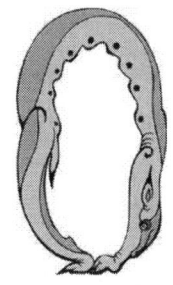

"TWO ARE BETTER THAN ONE, BECAUSE THEY HAVE A GOOD REWARD FOR THEIR LABOR. FOR IF THEY FALL, ONE WILL LIFT UP HIS COMPANION. BUT WOE TO HIM WHO IS ALONE WHEN HE FALLS, FOR HE HAS NO ONE TO HELP HIM UP."
~ECCLESIASTES 4:9,10

Ourselves or with Others?

I have met many homeschoolers over the last 20 years. Most of them have been enjoying their experiences, at least overall. But occasionally I meet someone who is not enjoying it, or who has given up altogether. And these homeschoolers usually have one thing in common – they are homeschooling <u>alone</u>. They do not have a support system. They are spending all day every day alone with their children. Now don't get me wrong, I love my children, and I spend a lot of time with them. But I depend on my support system. I need other moms to encourage me and to lift me up in prayer. God doesn't call us to carry our burdens alone.

When I think of homeschooling with others, four areas come to mind:

- Support Groups
- Co-ops
- Classes
- Homeschooling others' children with my own

Support Groups

When we began home schooling, home school support groups were in their infancy. When I moved to Germany, my first "support group" was one other family. We were both doing KONOS at home during the week, and then we went to the library together every Friday, and on regular field trips together.

When we moved to another part of Germany, I made a new friend who had moved recently from California. Cami had been in a good support group there and wanted something similar in the military community in our part of Germany. Since one didn't already exist, she was eager to start one! (Never mind that she was about to deliver her fourth child! She waited to have the first meeting till her son was a month old, and I came to the meeting to help out – straight from the hospital with my seventh child.)

We went on to begin what I believe was the first Germany-based American Home School Support Group (at least in our era). We immediately started with twice monthly Moms' Meetings and weekly Park Days. Regular field trips, craft classes, and theme parties quickly joined the schedule. And we went on to organize the first several American Curriculum Fairs in Germany.

And in all three Support Groups I've been active in, Moms' Meetings and Park Days have been a common element. Each group was unique in its focus, its size, and its role in our lives. But each provided critical support, that I can't imagine having homeschooled much longer without them. (Our first three years we were alone in our adventure – and I don't recommend that to anyone!) If there's no group nearby that meets your needs, consider starting one!

Co-ops

One of the ways I like to describe home schooling is "parent-directed education". Once we decide to home school, we can do ALL the teaching ourselves if we like, BUT we don't have to do it that way. One option that appeals to many is co-oping.

Perhaps, before we go any further, a definition would be appropriate. I define co-oping as simply "organized sharing of teaching responsibilities with two or more like-minded families". It can take many forms. There is no right or wrong way to co-op.

We have included co-oping in our educational "package" a number of times (during at least six school years at last count). Overall it has been quite enjoyable and educational. I would like to share some of the things we have experienced during the years we incorporated co-ops into our home school.

When we did this with more than one other family, we got together as moms before the start of the school year (sometimes at a Moms' overnight, but sometimes just at a park while the kids played nearby) and discussed our expectations for the co-op. We scheduled the upcoming activities and classes for the coming year. We also made sure we understood any particular needs or desires of the particular families involved. (For instance, Christmas topics are okay, Halloween topics are not, that type of thing.) If we actually planned something that one family wasn't comfortable with (which we tried not to do) -- they knew it in advance and could skip that week.

With all the co-ops our family has been involved with, we had one day each week set aside for our co-op. Some co-ops met for an entire school year, some met just for eight or ten weeks at a time. In one co-op, we didn't divide into age groups at all. With our other, smaller co-ops we only had two age divisions – the "younger kids" and the "older kids". That year we had six families participating – each week one mom led each division, one mom helped in each division, and two moms had the week "off" – and they could either take the day off, "watch", or help in one of the two classes. In a more recent co-op, which included more than a dozen families, we had a nursery, and four different age groups. When we had our planning meetings, we figured out who would be responsible for each age for each week. We also divided teaching responsibilities: in some groups, who was teaching varied from week to week; in some it stayed the same for the entire co-op.

These co-ops have helped us share educational experiences with our children that they might not have otherwise had. They took music, Spanish, and other classes that I didn't feel as comfortable teaching, while I shared astronomy and thinking skills with families that might have missed those topics in their "package" for the year. We all benefited from the arrangement. We blessed each other, and we blessed our families.

With each coop we tried to keep costs down – some were free, others have had small registration fees and very small class fees (to cover expenses). Some have met in churches, some in community centers, and smaller ones even in homes.

Classes with other homeschoolers

Many homeschoolers are seeing the benefit of formal classes for some portion of the school day or week. With these classes, we can still maintain the benefits of home schooling – low student/teacher ratio and direct parent involvement. And we can take advantage of the strengths of other teaching parents.

We were a number of years into our homeschooling experience before we started doing occasional classes with other homeschoolers. The first time, one of the dads in our support group with a science background offered to do a weekly high school Biology lab in his home. (That took care of dissection for my oldest two – I was thrilled, even if they weren't.) Soon after that I offered a history class for upper elementary and junior high students. We met once a week in my home. It was wonderful – we spent an entire year studying the Revolutionary War. One of my friends reciprocated with a science class for the junior high students, and another friend kept an eye on the younger kids during the two hour class. We all enjoyed the arrangement immensely.

Outside of co-ops, I have also taught classes about U.S. Presidents, Shakespeare, Thinking Skills, and the U.S. Constitution. Some of the classes have been free – and for some I charge $2/class. (I don't get rich that way – but it covers most of my expenses!) My kids have also taken French, Spanish, Science (lots!), Economics, Music, and Math classes with other homeschool moms. Again, some of those have been free, and some have not.

Classes are a great way to meet the needs of any age students, in almost any subject. We usually fill ours through direct "word of mouth", and sometimes through "the power of the internet"!

Teaching Other People's Children Full-time

Before we leave this chapter, this is one other area we should discuss – taking full responsibility for the education of someone else's child(ren). Some would consider this tutoring, and some counsel not to do this, under any circumstances. I disagree with both of these counsels. It is certainly not something to be entered into quickly, but rather prayerfully and cautiously, since it is a big commitment.

Our first experience with this was only three years into our homeschooling adventure. A couple that my husband worked with had a son about the same age as our older two (all three were doing third grade work). The parents heard we were teaching our children at home (a rare thing in those days) and approached us about Joe joining us for school for the first semester of that school year. We prayed about it, talked about it, and agreed. Every morning (Monday through Friday) Joe's mom or dad dropped him off on their way to work, and every day at lunch time picked him up again (except field trip days, when he stayed with us for the entire day). It worked well, he did well, and we all enjoyed that semester. We didn't use any textbooks, other than math. (That was our first KONOS year.)

In January we were preparing to move, and yes, the military had okayed Joe's attendance at their school for the second semester. Great! Wonderful! But wait: There was a snag. Since he had not been "in school" that first semester, the school wanted to put him back in second grade for the remainder of the year. I was invited to come to the school to explain why he should be allowed to finish third grade. I showed up at the appointed hour – expecting to meet with two or three school personnel. Imagine my surprise when I was ushered into a room with a dozen school professionals, only one of whom had even heard of homeschooling before. I presented a brief summary of how we had conducted our school, what we had studied, the field trips we had gone on, etc. By time I finished, Joe was accepted into the third grade and they were telling me they had other students they could send my way! I respectfully declined. Joe went on to finish the school year with A's and B's, instead of the C's and D's he had been getting the years before. We have no regrets about the decision to include him in our home school that semester.

Many, many years later we were privileged to have first one, and then two, of my nieces live and school with us for a time. Those were also good experiences, and I was thrilled to stand up with my sister and my niece at her graduation a couple of years ago. She has gone on to college where she is doing well. It was a blessing for us to participate in her home education, and that of her sister.

Conclusion

Home schooling is an educational package directed by the parents. It does not have to be done completely within the confines of your house, with just you and your children. Please do not try to home school "alone". Prayerfully seek out the others God would put you with – and consider how you will encourage each other – whether it be though co-ops or classes or Moms' Meetings or "just" prayer.

> "I NEVER LET SCHOOLING INTERFERE WITH MY EDUCATION."
> MARK TWAIN

Philosophy of Education

Philosophy of Education

"Philosophy of Education" has quickly become a passion for me. Consequently, this chapter has taken on a life of its own. The early notes for it spanned dozens of pages. But that's more than seemed necessary for a chapter in this book. Someday, I'd like to write a booklet just on this topic, but in the meantime, if this chapter leaves you wanting to read more, there are three specific books I can recommend now: *The Simplicity of Homeschooling* by Vicky Goodchild; *Education, Christianity, and the State* by J. Gresham Machen; and *Christian Philosophy of Education* by Gordon H. Clark. The second and third books are heavier reading and don't specifically deal with home education, but they are excellent! It would do home educators good to pay more attention to them.

For as important a subject as this is, it is too widely ignored in home school circles. We often make decisions on curriculum without really considering our own philosophy of education.

As I've worked to distill my notes on this subject, I've come up with a few basic questions that beg asking as we consider: What is our philosophy of education? How do we determine it? What difference should it make?

Let's start with the standard reporting questions: Who?; What?; Where?; Why?; When?; How? But bear with me, please, as I switch the order around a bit.

What:
Let's start here:
- <u>What</u> is your worldview?
- <u>What</u> is a philosophy of education?
- <u>What</u> is *my* philosophy of education?
- More importantly, <u>what</u> is *your* philosophy of education?
- <u>What</u> are your goals? <u>What</u> are the ends you have in mind?
- <u>What</u> is an educated person?

<u>What is your worldview?</u> Even before you can consider philosophies of education, you need to consider your views of the world and life. What role does God play in your world? What role does He play in your life? From those basic questions, you can begin to consider the specifics of education, and how it impacts your family.

<u>What is a philosophy of education</u>: I define it as: "the ideas, constraints, and goals that determine how we should be training our children for life." Actually that definition gives away some of my own philosophy, but so be it. You may come up with a definition you like better.

Notice this definition does not include the word "school". Repeat after me: "School does not equal education; education does not equal school." We may use the words interchangeably sometimes, speaking of "home school" and "home education", but the words are *not* equivalent. School is "an <u>organization</u> that provides <u>instruction</u>";[70] education is "the development of <u>knowledge</u>, <u>skill</u>, <u>ability</u>, or <u>character</u> by teaching, training, study, or experience".[71] In other words, education goes so much beyond schooling. We would do well to remember that. This definition also mentions life as an end objective, not a diploma. But more on diplomas later.

<u>My own philosophy of education</u> is revealed throughout this book. But if I were to try to sum it up, it might best be said as simply: "God has given parents the right and the responsibility to train their children through life and for life." The decisions my husband and I make in educating our children should be consistent with our philosophy.

<u>What is your philosophy of education?</u> Are you trying to bring school home? Are you trying to get your students through graduation? Into college? Do you want to make them better kids? Better adults? These are the kinds of questions you need to ask yourself. You don't need to have all the answers right away, but the idea is to start thinking. If you don't have some of these answers, how can you be making decisions on what to use in your home school?

<u>What are your goals?</u> <u>What are the ends you have in mind?</u> Additionally, we want to think about <u>what</u> we should be teaching. <u>What</u> do our children need? An education that will serve them well in life. An education that is balanced. Plenty to think about, since "it's impossible to think with an empty mind."[72]

---

[70] According to the Merriam Webster Collegiate Dictionary, copyright 1998
[71] According to the World Book Dictionary, copyright 1988
[72] Education, Christianity, and the State, pg 7

<u>What is an educated person?</u> *My answer would include:*
- One who <u>knows and loves God</u>
- One who knows <u>how to learn</u>
- One who <u>loves learning</u>
- One who <u>reads well</u>
- One who <u>writes well</u>
- One who <u>speaks well</u>
- One who is <u>proficient in math</u>

Who:

<u>Who</u> has the primary responsibility of training children? Parents!

<u>Who</u> should educate their children at home? Well, who <u>shouldn't?</u> Since their education is already a God-given responsibility, parents are making a decision <u>not</u> to educate their children at home, not the other way around![73]

I actually think home education might better be called "parent-directed learning", but my son has pointed out that <u>parenting</u> *is* parent-directed learning. So isn't <u>parenting</u> the equivalent to home educating? Or at least, shouldn't it be?

<u>Who</u> should be making the decisions about what's best for their students? Dad and mom, with some occasional, appropriate input from their kids. (Read: Dad and Mom, *not* the government.)

Why:

<u>Why</u> should you educate your children at home? *Why not?* This really goes hand in hand with what your philosophy of education is, and who you believe has the responsibility for your children.

---

[73] Whether it's a conscious decision or not.

Do we want to do this because we believe children learn better at home? Better with a smaller teacher/student ratio? Better when we control the curriculum? Because they'll be better socialized? (Seriously, see my answer to this oft-asked question in the *Questions and Answers* chapter.) Because we want to disciple them?[74] These are just a few of the reasons we should be educating our children at home! Just be sure you understand these and other reasons you may have.

And if you want some good reasons NOT to send your kids to the government run schools, look at any of the books John Taylor Gatto has written. Mr. Gatto taught for years in New York, and was New York City and State Teacher of the Year between 1989 - 1991[75] before he finally quit teaching in disgust. If you are determined *not* to home school, don't read his books, especially *Dumbing Us Down*.

Where:
Well, since we're "home educating" our children, home is certainly a good place to begin. But it doesn't have to be just at home. We have lots of other options. (See the *Others* chapter for many of those options.) Our high school students can also be taking some of their classes at a local college for dual credit, our students can be apprenticing at dad's work or somewhere else. We can frequent museums and other wonderful places for exciting hands-on or 3-dimensional learning. (See the *Zoos and Museums* chapter for more on that.)

We should be directing our children's education. We do not necessarily have to be doing it all ourselves, and certainly not all within the confines of our own home. (Of course, on the

---

[74] Not just discipline them – though both are necessary!
[75] He was New York City Teacher of the year all three years, and New York State Teacher of the Year in 1990 and 1991.

other hand, we <u>can</u> be doing it all, by ourselves, at home! It' our choice. What is God calling <u>us</u> to do for <u>our</u> children?)

When:
From right now until graduation sounds good to me! But I don't know your situation, so that really is a flippant answer. When we first began, we were taking it "one year at a time". It wasn't until we had been at this 10 years that we finally became committed to "the long haul". Only you and God know what will work for your family. There are some home schooling families that even do *college* at home. Thus far we haven't gone that route…But maybe you will.

How:
The <u>how</u> of home educating is where things get really complicated these days. There are almost too many choices. Ultimately, you need to do what works for your family. And remember, the methods are merely a means to an end.

Entire books are written on the many options available, so I won't repeat that information here. Instead, I'll merely mention the main methods, and give you a taste of our experiences with each of these. (*The Simplicity of Homeschooling* does a great job of going into the highlights of each; that would be a great place to look for more details on any of them.) We've actually used each of these to varying degrees in our home over the years:

<u>Range of Options:</u>
- Unschooling

John Holt was one of the first to write on this subject. After attempting to "reform" the schools, Holt had given up on that, and attempted to bring children to their full potential "outside" the world of schools instead. We had read several of his books before our first child was even born; he influenced us significantly in our early years.

- Relaxed Homeschooling

Mary Hood coined this term a few years back; it was like a breath of fresh air to us. It brought us the balance between unschooling and textbooks.

- Unit Studies

Unit studies often attempt to do more of a "hands on" approach to homeschooling, typically incorporating many subjects into one study. There are many unit studies that can be bought and used straight "out of the box". KONOS was the first – and we were among the first families to enjoy it when it hit the early homeschooling market. Many other quality products have followed as well.

- Living Books

Charlotte Mason wrote and taught more than a hundred years ago. She advocated "real books" or "living books", instead of textbooks. She also recommended nature studies, art and music appreciation, and Shakespeare. I would recommend starting with one of the many guides to Charlotte Mason, not her own books. Hers are very good, but very difficult to read.

- Classical Education

Doug Wilson is one of the advocates of classical education in the Christian community. In Classical teaching the emphasis is on the Trivium, which consists of Grammar, Dialectic, and Rhetoric. The part of it we incorporate the most is the emphasis on logic.

- Textbooks

Bob Jones, A Beka, Christian Liberty Press are just a few of the Christian textbook publishers these days. And of course there are plenty of secular publishing companies to choose from. We have used more than a handful of these, particularly in our early years. (I'll save my opinion on textbooks for other places!)

- Correspondence School

American School and Christian Liberty Academy are the only correspondence schools my family has actually used. My older son gave American School a definite "thumbs down", though my oldest daughter was very happy with it.

Overlapping these Options:
- Better Late than Early

Dr. Raymond and Dorothy Moore warned that we should not start our children's formal education too soon, before they were physically mature enough.

- Games

Games can and should be used as a supplement no matter which method(s) we primarily use. Because games are fun, and easy to repeat, and three-dimensional, they reinforce learning in a way that's hard to replicate with other methods. (More on those in the *Fun, History,* and *"3 R's"* chapters.)

- Hands-On/Experiments

For some students hands-on learning will be very important. For all students it can add another dimension to lessons to spice things up. Don't get caught up in **having** to have a lot of these – but feel free to, if it fits into your family's lifestyle.[76]

---

[76] In other words, our family **doesn't** do many science experiments.

Within these Options:

Choosing the "curriculum" we will use can be one of the most intimidating parts of our homeschooling journal. Curriculum is a very broad term. It is often used to describe what I call the "canned" stuff – textbooks and workbooks and teachers' manuals – that resemble what most of us did in our school years.

But in our home education options, the meaning of the word goes far beyond that. Our curriculum is what we use, <u>how</u> we teach, <u>how</u> we accomplish this process of educating our children. It may or may not include textbooks, it may or may not include computers, but it certainly needs to reflect our philosophy of education.

How many decisions do we make for our students' education because they're what we're comfortable with? Because it's what we know? Because it's easy?

We've already made the biggest break with current "tradition" by bringing our children home, by being willing to take control of their education. Let's not stop there. Let's not duplicate a failing public school system.

The advantages which we have in home education go far beyond the low student/teacher ratio. They go beyond our ability to include rather than exclude our Christian beliefs. (Those are both important, they're just not the only reasons we homeschool.) We should turn our back on a monumental educational experiment that has dominated the American scene for 150 years.

I did not realize until I attended a recent curriculum fair that there are still so many home schoolers who truly do "school at home". At this particular fair I would estimate that at least 200 of the 300 parents present made a bee-line to the major curriculum vendors. I cringed to watch the thousands of dollars beings so carelessly spent – I cringed to think of the bondage being bought, the tears that would follow. Am I being harsh? Yes. Am I being too harsh? I don't believe so. Those home schoolers too often will be the ones who will burn out, who will wonder what they're doing, who will put their kids back in school, who will blame their home schooling problems on the <u>home</u> rather than the <u>schooling</u>.

Some hands-on learning at Fort Mandan, North Dakota.

Too many times we choose our curriculum based on what our friends are using, or on the latest educational fad, or simply on what sounds best at a Curriculum Fair. That's a really a shame. This is one of the most important steps in the educational process – choosing the material we plan to use to help our children learn. We will make mistakes in our choices, no doubt about it. (That's one of the reasons we have used book sales, after all!) But it is beneficial for all involved if we can minimize our mistakes.

A major problem with canned curriculum is that it is not individualized. Education is NOT a "one size fits all" t-shirt. How does a textbook publisher know what my student needs to study in third grade? Or is ready to study? And what about those of us with multiple age students? Try using canned curriculum on three different levels at a time. (Never mind, *don't* try it. Talk about a quick road to insanity. Just take my word for it, it's not fun! And look at the *Multi-level Teaching* chapter if you need more information on better options in that situation.)

And what about those of us with slow learners? Not every child is "above average". Or advanced learners? Or those who have an unusual interest? What are we doing to ourselves and our families when we let someone else dictate what we will study and when we will study it? Who knows our children and their needs better than we do, after all? That's why many of us began this task in the first place. We wanted to meet the needs of our children. And yet, we'll turn around and put ourselves under the bondage of textbooks.

Now, if you are currently using textbooks, and currently think they are the most wonderful thing in the world, please hear me out....Are they meeting the needs of your child(ren)? Are they really working for you? Well, if they are, then by all means keep it up. But if they're not, then why not consider your options? And if *you* like them, but your *students* don't, then what? If they are resisting textbooks, it doesn't mean they are resisting learning. Oftentimes we need to blame the materials, not the students! Remember, there are many wonderful materials out there, waiting for us to use.

"But that requires some effort," you say. Well, yes, it does. But if you weren't willing to put some effort into this task, your students would probably still be in the public school system, wouldn't they? And it's not that teaching with textbooks requires no effort at all. I'm just suggesting that you redirect some of that energy.

Education comes in different shapes and sizes.

Summary

As you prayerfully consider your many options for <u>how</u> to home educate, and make your curriculum choices, remember these important thoughts:

- There is a difference between knowledge and wisdom. We want to raise wise children, not just smart ones;
- True education is teaching children how to learn and to love learning;
- We need to model learning for our students – do we love learning? Do we demonstrate a passion for it?
- We must train our children to use their minds. ("Thou shalt love the Lord thy God with all thy heart and soul and mind."[77])
- Just as we learn when God repeats things for us, our children will learn through repetition. "Precept upon precept…line upon line…here a little there a little."[78] And the more they see it, hear it, say it, and do it, the more they will remember.

---

[77] Deuteronomy 6:5
[78] Isaiah 28:9, 10

> "JUDGE A MAN BY HIS QUESTIONS
> RATHER THAN BY HIS ANSWERS."
> VOLTAIRE

Questions and Answers

(Some of the questions I usually hear about home education, and my best attempts at answering them)

Is it Legal?
What about Socialization?
What about High School?
What about College?
What about Tests?
What about Standardized Tests?
What about Gaps in their Learning?
My husband only approves of Textbooks. Now what?
How important are Learning Styles?
How about Schedules?
What about Grandparents?
How do we do it all?
What do we do about Foreign Languages?
Can this be done on a Tight Budget?

Q: Is it <u>Legal</u>?

A: This used to be the most common question I heard. After 20 years, I don't hear it as often, but occasionally it still surfaces. Today's answer {in the United States} is generally "Yes, with some restrictions, home schooling is legal in all 50 states." Unfortunately even in the short time I've been working on this book, problems have arisen in several states. So this situation may change at any time. {And of course, sadly, in the international community, there are a number of countries which do not allow homeschooling. For instance, when we lived in Germany twenty years ago it was difficult for Germans to homeschool, and I understand that the situation there has not improved. Our hearts and prayers go out for those who are not allowed to educate their children fully at home, and we ask blessings on those who are looking for creative ways to supplement what their children learn in their "public school" settings – both in the United States and in other countries.}

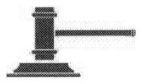

Q: What about <u>Socialization</u>?

A: One of my favorite anti-home schooling questions has to be this one. To which I would have to ask in response: Is that the goal of schools? Is that the role of schools? Does my failure to participate in "formal schooling" truly limit the ability of my children to be socialized? I would answer NO to all of those questions. Socialization does not occur when children spend most of their waking hours in a group situation with dozens of their peers. Socialization occurs when children learn how to relate to those who are younger, as well as to those who are older; to relate to those who are different from them, as well as those who are similar to them. True socialization includes the ability to relate to adults as well. Where does all this socialization take place naturally? In a home, not a school. Particularly in large families. Believe me, socialization is not a problem at my house! In fact, a recent study in Vancouver, Canada showed that home educated students as a group are "better socialized than their peers."[79]

Now, if the real question is, "what about <u>time</u> with their peers?" Then, yes, we do provide for that too. Our children participate in many activities with peers – Boy Scouts and home school classes being at the top of the list. Believe me, time WITH their peers is not a problem. But our time with peers is *controlled* time. There is adequate adult supervision. There is a purpose for the "peer time", and there is still adequate time home with family. Those all lead to true socialization.

The bigger concern is, how are "schooled" students being properly socialized?

Q: What about <u>High School</u>?

A: It is a shame to me that so many home schoolers still worry about teaching high school at home. I know when my oldest got to that age 11 years ago, I was concerned. But at that point, so few had gone before us. Now I do not fret about the high school years, but rather look forward to them. I'll go into more details in the *Teaching Teens* chapter.

---

[79] Quoted in *Christianity Today*, December 2001, on page 17

Q: What about College?
A: College admission is not a problem for home educated students who desire to go to college.

I want my children to be academically, emotionally, and spiritually prepared to go to college, if that's the direction God is leading them. But college is not necessarily right for each of them, and oftentimes "delayed college" is the right answer. Like the other major (and minor) decisions in their lives, this is one that should only be approached prayerfully and carefully.

Very few colleges discriminate against home-educated students anymore. In fact, many colleges are looking for home-educated applicants, because they realize what an asset they can be to the school.

Many factors go into the college admissions process – grades, standardized test scores, recommendations, essays, and much more. Home-educated students are typically not at a disadvantage for getting into college! And if for some reason, they do not have the scores to get into the four-year college of their choice initially, junior colleges are a good way for them to "prove themselves" in the college world.

Our family is not opposed to our children going to college, but we are also not opposed to them NOT going to college. A couple of the older ones have started college straight out of our home school high school, but most of them have not. Of our first four high school graduates, they have all had some college, but only one will have started and finished college straight out of high school. (And he has done it in three years, instead of four!)

Q: What about <u>Tests</u>?
A: Tests are another concern for some people when they consider using a more relaxed method of schooling. "What about tests," they ask? "What about them?" I usually answer. Tests are not really necessary in most home school situations. They help classroom teachers figure out what 20 – 30 students are comprehending on any number of subjects. Home schoolers do not have that same need. Even with seven students I can tell by our discussions what my students know. Test if you want to, but it's not a great loss if you don't. (How many of us remember cramming for tests in high school and college – how much of that do you remember???) Beyond math, what purpose do most tests serve in a home school situation, anyway?

> "Testing will come later – in life."[80]
> Dr. Llewellyn Cook

Q: What about <u>Standardized Tests</u>?
A: Standardized tests are an obnoxious part of most of our lives. As I mentioned above, they are a part of getting into college much of the time. So we do pay some attention to standardized tests in our home education system – we typically make our students endure one, sometime in their high school years. We don't really find them to be necessary

---
[80] Dr. Llewellyn Cook, 28 June 2002 (*Ancient Egypt* talk)

beyond that, so we don't bother with them any more often than that. In fact, I would not willingly join a group that required annual standardized testing. To that requirement I can only ask, what's the point? In fact, I might also ask if we stop to think about the premise behind standardized tests in the first place. "When you are dealing with human beings standardization is the last thing you ought to seek...Standardization destroys the personal character of human life."[81] Precisely my point!

If you have a student who is a good test taker, the PSAT during their 10th and 11th grade years will be helpful – it is the key to many scholarships.[82]

Most colleges require the ACT and some require the SAT and SAT 2s. We try to stick to the absolute minimum.

Q: What about <u>Gaps in their Learning</u>?
A: Yes, those will exist. They will exist regardless of the method of education employed.

Our goals should include, teaching our children to:
- Love God/Obey parents
- Read and enjoy reading
- Be excited about learning
- Understand research options

The specific details contained in their "curriculum package" are not really the issue. Are we setting the foundation? If we accomplish these things – what difference will the gaps make? If a gap exists in an area that is really important, it will

---

[81] *Education, Christianity, and the State*, pgs 74, 103
[82] One of my sons almost all of his college paid for because of his PSAT scores.

show up, and then it can be dealt with. If it wasn't important for that student, why does it matter? And remember, a student who "covers" an entire "gap-free" textbook in one year has seldom *learned* much of it anyway!

Q: My <u>husband only approves of Textbooks</u>. Now what?
A: This is one of the most serious questions to deal with and it needs to be resolved in a win/win way. Not a compromise, so much as a new approach. What about using the textbooks – but using them a little differently than the "right" way? For instance, use *one* history textbook for two students who are close together in age, instead of two different books. And what about supplementing the textbook with other materials, and not trying to cover the entire book in one year? Those two changes may help relax the home school pressures, and are often enough to relieve Dad's concerns.

Q: How important are <u>Learning Styles</u>?
A: Learning styles are important to a point, particularly if a student is struggling with a subject. If a student isn't learning to read for instance, we may want to consider how that student learns best. Is he an auditory learner, a visual learner, or a hands-on learner? If we focus more on his "style", we may help him overcome some obstacles.

But beyond a "problem area", we shouldn't focus too much on learning styles. It's better for students to get used to learning with various styles, than it is to focus on a particular one. Visual, auditory, and hands-on methods can all reinforce each other, rather than one being chosen at the exclusion of the others.

Q: How about <u>Schedules</u>?
A: What we practice in our home probably best resembles the "flex-time" schedules that many work places now employ. We have a rough idea of how each day should look, and how each week generally flows. But we have a lot of freedom within that framework for variances. If we have a late night for some reason (company, a play we all attended, or whatever), we can sleep in the next morning if we need to, and just adjust our expectations. If an unscheduled field trip comes up that we're just dying to do, the day's plans can always wait until another time. I am in control of our schedule, it is not in control of me.

Additionally, a chore chart does make keeping up with household duties easier. "Whose turn is to wash the dishes?" "Who's making dinner tonight?" A schedule can answer these questions quickly.

One of the things that has helped both our scheduling and our sanity has been to rethink how we approach the "typical" schooling week. Instead of trying to get to each subject every day, like we were used to doing in school, why not designate certain days for certain subjects? Why not English on one day, history on another, and science on yet another? That way I can concentrate my preparation on one subject at a time, instead of many; and we can more easily fit school and life into the same week! When I made that change many years back, I was amazed at the freedom that it brought to our scheduling, and our schooling.

Another important change, was scheduling the bulk of school for the mornings – without lots of busywork, it's amazing how fast the real work can be accomplished! "Productive free time"[83] fills most of my kids' afternoons. It's important for our children to have some unstructured time in their day – for solitude – for independent reading – for educational fun. Let's work hard to not over-structure their days!

Q: What about <u>Grandparents</u>?
A: Supportive grandparents are certainly a blessing, but some grandparents take to the idea of their grandchildren being home educated easier than others do. Time will usually bring them around. When they start seeing the positive results, most are easily convinced. (If they're still adamant about their objections, maybe you can get them a good book to read about the subject…If they still have a problem, I recommend that you leave it in God's hands, and just be in regular prayer about it.)

---

[83] Reading and playing with Legos are the two biggest afternoon activities. Roller blading and running around outside in the yard are close behind.

Q: How do we <u>do it all</u>?
A: We don't…Maybe I should have started with this one, since it is a question that I am often asked. Repeat after me, "We don't do it all! We can't do it all! We shouldn't do it all." There are only 24-hours in each day, and we really need to slow down and <u>enjoy</u> some of them.

I personally do a very limited amount of housework – my children wash the dishes, do most of the laundry, sweep, vacuum, and…I guess you get the picture. I do wash laundry about once a week, for my husband and me. That's all the laundry I personally take care of. (And there have been times when I have even delegated that…catch that important word, please – DELEGATION. A very important word in any home schooling mom's vocabulary.) When I'm really organized, I even have my kids cook most of the meals. These are all-important skills for our kids to learn. My older kids have all been shocked as they've left home and been around peers who don't know how to do these basic things because they never did them at home. Mine leave home confident that they can take care of themselves in all these mundane areas. Work should be an integral part of our children's life (even before they appreciate that fact). Life is about balance, and sometimes we moms feel very much out of balance. But maybe that's because we need to give more of it up to God. We can't do it all, and we need to stop trying so hard!

Q: What do we do about <u>Foreign Languages</u> for our students, if we are not bi-lingual or just don't feel comfortable in this area?
A: Foreign Language is often considered a critical but difficult subject to get taken care of in our home school settings. There are many subjects I have felt fine learning <u>with</u> my students – but not this one. Consequently, we've

had to work harder to get this done. In fact two of my three older students have lamented the lack of foreign language they had before graduating. I actually tried to do classes in Spanish for them using two different homeschooling programs. We never got through either of them. I take the credit for that lack, I do not blame the programs in this case. Since I am not very fluent in Spanish, teaching it to my children was a constant struggle.

Fortunately, their lack of credits in that area did not keep them out of college when they applied, but it could certainly hurt in some cases. One of them eventually did take Spanish at the university she was attending. And another one learned Albanian when he went to Albania as a missionary. (Now there's a good way to learn a language!)

On the mission field in Mexico. Nine of my 15 children/daughter-in-laws have done short term and long term mission work at this point.

My fourth and fifth students studied German and Spanish on their own one year, using some materials we tried first at the library, and then bought at a local book store. That gave them each a good introduction to the languages, but it's tough to get far that way.

My fourth student then took Russian at a local college, while a senior in high school. This gave him both high school and college credit. He did very well, and that worked for him.

My next three sons had the opportunity to take French with another mom who was teaching a French class for local homeschoolers with PowerGlide. Two of them ended up taking two years of French with her. That worked well for them.

As you can see, there are lots of options for taking care of Foreign Language requirements. You can find the solution for your family out there.

Q: Can this be done on a <u>Tight budget</u>?
A: Certainly! Materials cost money, but we can survive a tight home schooling budget by
- Buying less
- Borrowing more[84] (too often overlooked as an option!)
- Being ever diligent in looking for "educational freebies".[85]
- Shopping wisely.

I'll deal with this more in the *Saving Money* chapter, but I wanted to assure those on a tight budget that home schooling does not have to add a further strain.

In Conclusion
I don't claim to have all the answers; I'm still asking many of the questions myself. In fact, many times, I think the best answer to a question is another question. But may some of these questions and answers help you get started.

---

[84] Materials can often be borrowed from friends, acquaintances, and of course, public libraries.
[85] There are many free resources out there: County Extension Offices, State Tourist offices and many rest areas (maps, informative brochures, etc.). [And of course, now, the Internet.]

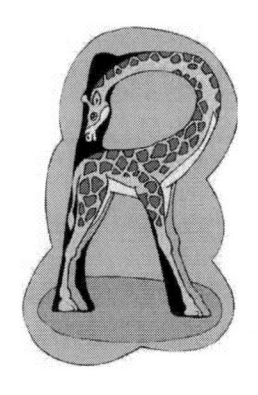

"THERE ARE ONLY TWO POWERS IN THE WORLD
THE SWORD AND THE PEN;
AND IN THE END THE FORMER IS ALWAYS
CONQUERED BY THE LATTER."
NAPOLEON BONAPARTE

The 3 R's :
Reading, wRiting, and aRithmetic

Reading

I often wonder if we forget what the main goal of our Reading programs should be – to teach our children to read; and to give them a love of reading. Until we have accomplished both of these, nothing else matters much in our English programs![86]

I am often asked which Phonics program is the best. I haven't used them all, but I've certainly tried more than "my fair share" of them (seven at last count!). When all is said and done, none of them were clear winners in my book (I guess that's part of the reason I've tried so many!), but they all

---

[86] And yes, I'm referring to Spelling, Grammar, Composition, and the list goes on.

accomplished the job in the end – teaching the child to read, and from there, to read well. Since that was the objective, I can't really complain about any of them.

Phonics – the idea is to teach them to read! Please **don't** lose sight of that. Good readers actually sight-read; once they learn to read, constant use of phonics just slows them down. Phonics is the easiest way to teach most students the mechanics of reading, but learning phonics is not the goal, learning to <u>read</u> well <u>is</u>. Any phonics work we have our students do should only bring them closer to that goal.

Once a child can read, we dispense with the phonics program in our home, and we practice reading, reading, and more reading – all in real books, many of them of the student's choosing, and many of my choosing. We don't do "readers" – we read books. Please see the difference before you go on! And, if you didn't start the book at this chapter, it probably won't come as a big surprise to you that we don't generally do book reports or use comprehension questions either. Not that an occasional book report or an occasional set of questions would be so terrible, but if either of these frustrate your new reader, they are not worth it! Go back to the first premise – English programs should be turning out readers who read well, and enjoy reading. Anything that doesn't help us get to that goal should be scrapped quickly!

In fact, I'm losing patience with the increasing number of literature "guides" that are on the market now. Do we really need these? What do they really accomplish? Must we dissect good literature to make it better? Must we ask and answer endless questions about the books we read? Children need interaction <u>with</u> good literature, not <u>about</u> it! If you really want your children to enjoy the reading that they do – stick to some basic questions, like: "What part did you like best?" "What would you have changed?" "What was the author trying to get across?" Why dissect a good book beyond that?

Thus far, we have turned out eight accomplished readers among my students, and the next two are not far behind. In this house, the usual command is, "Put the book down and finish your chores" or your other work, or whatever the case may be. Getting books *into* the hands of those who enjoy reading is not the problem, it's getting them *out* once in a while!

Another note, especially in the area of reading: We are in the "Better Late Than Early" camp with Raymond and Dorothy Moore. We do not start the reading process at five or six. We generally start phonics closer to seven or eight, possibly even nine. And once we've started, it generally goes quickly.

My children usually go from being non-readers to accomplished readers in six to eight months. And when I say accomplished, I'm talking about reading well above grade level, with the ability to read and comprehend most classic literature by age ten. I ran across this interesting fact recently:

"In 1683, Pennsylvania law required that anyone teaching children had to ensure those children could read and write by age 12."[87] I don't believe the current trend toward pushing reading at increasingly lower ages has been a good thing! I do have a 10-year-old who is still working on the basics of reading – but I am quite confident that she will read well long before age 12!

Just for the sake of example, let me share a sample of the books my last 9-year-old read (and understood and enjoyed) one spring, just six months after getting the hang of reading – *Jungle Book*, *Robin Hood*, *King Arthur*, and *Oliver Twist* (all the unabridged versions, by the way!). His 11-year-old brother read each of those, and *Journey to the Center of the Earth*, *Watership Down*, and Tolkien's *Lord of the Rings* series, during the same time period.

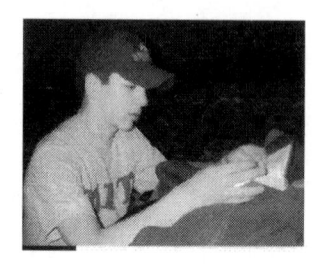

Now, before I go on, I want to share an exception to the above pattern. I did have one of my older students who started reading between seven and eight, but by his eleventh birthday, he still did not particularly **enjoy** reading. He did it when he had to, but certainly no more than that. And mainly because he did not practice much, his proficiency did not improve.

But all was not lost. Right around his eleventh birthday, we got a card in the mail for a marvelous new series – *The American Adventures*. At that time the only way to buy them

---

[87] Gormley

was through the mail, two books each month, for two years. (Now they can be found in Christian bookstores and in many of the home school catalogs.) We started getting the set, and in almost no time, his desire to read had increased, and with it, his ability to read. By time he finished the series two years later, he had truly become proficient at reading, and now reads adult-level books with the best of them.

And lest we forget, the principle reason for early schools in this country was so that children could learn to read the Bible. "The College curriculum was to be the culmination of a Christian education that began at birth. The first textbook printed in North America was the New England Primer. Its first line was 'In Adam's fall, we sinned all.'"[88]

I think that most of us would agree that: "Indispensable to everyone is the ability to read."[89] And yet we must remember even so that reading is "just another tool". Must of our children will learn to read well, and should get to where they enjoy reading. But not all of them will; just as all of our children will not be "above average", they will not all "fall in love with reading". Some have learning disabilities that truly make reading a chore; others just have different interests. We should teach them to read, we should work to ensure that they read well, but we must remember that not all of them read as much or as well as we might like. That's okay.

---

[88] *Trinity Review*, June 2000, Path to the Future, pg 2
[89] *A Christian Philosophy of Education*, pg 161

Ultimately, we need to ask, "Why do we want them to read?" So they can read and study the Bible? The Bible is available on tapes and CD's now. So that they can learn? Learning opportunities abound in other forms – video and audio both, for instance. So they can be aquatinted with the important people of the past? Maybe they should be getting aquatinted with some of the people of today – face to face. I say all this merely to point out that while I want my students to read well, and we work hard to accomplish that goal, all is not lost if they are not all avid readers.

Some of the "Reading" games and activities we enjoy include:
- *Scrabble, especially Speed Scrabble*
- *Boggle*
- *Crossword Puzzles*[90]
- *Apples to Apples*

These and others like them increase awareness of the English Language, in relatively painless ways.

Writing
There are lots of curriculums available if you feel the need to teach your children writing as a separate subject. But the biggest objective is to get them to write. In which case, they must feel like they have something worth writing about. That won't happen if we expect them to write too much, too soon.

I don't believe in giving younger students major writing assignments at all. I believe that typically leads to frustration.

---

[90] I had bought a Crossword Puzzle book recently as a gift. We didn't end up giving it, and it got left laying around for awhile. I "caught" my two high schoolers many times over the next few weeks working the puzzles in it – improving their vocabularies without even realizing it.

Even older students do better when they are writing in a context – for a purpose. Pen pals, emails, old fashioned thank you letters work well to increase their writing skills now, and as they get older the "real" opportunities will increase. For all ages, copywork is valuable.

Copywork

Cindy Rushton (*Language Arts the Easy Way*) and Ruth Beechick (*You Can Teach Your Child Successfully*) both do a great job of explaining copywork – so I won't belabor the point. But briefly, the idea is that kids copy increasingly larger passages of good literature. Through the copying they practice handwriting, good spelling, good grammar, and see the beauty of good writing. That all helps later when they are ready for original writing.

Just like artists copy the masters to improve, our students can copy good writing into a journal or notebook to improve their writing. They can see, read, and write good writing. There will be plenty of time for original writing later!

Handwriting

Handwriting ranks as somewhat important in my mind – it's nice for our students to have legible handwriting. But I personally have dreadful handwriting (and that was with years of work on it in schools!) – so I don't stress out too much over my children's handwriting. I have a personal preference for Italic writing over standard print and cursive, and actually teach it to my students occasionally. Copywork helps handwriting as much as anything else I've found.

Spelling

We don't use a separate spelling program anymore. We did early on, but I've grown increasingly frustrated with the ones I've tried. (My good spellers didn't need them, and my poor spellers didn't improve dramatically! So what was the point?) When my students write on the computer – they are allowed to use the spell checker (just as I use it). And they are encouraged to have someone proofread any major writing assignments. (I do that as an adult, so why do I want to offer less to them?)

Grammar

I don't suppose it will surprise anyone when I say at this point that I don't teach grammar as a separate subject either. We really have tried. But I have found that my children learn grammar better in context, through conversation and good literature. If I want them to learn some specific grammar terms (noun, verb, etc.), we do a couple of silly stories from a *Mad Libs* book, and they catch on very quickly.

Arithmetic

Math has been the one holdout for the use of textbooks for most of our homeschooling years. We had bought the idea that textbooks were the best way, perhaps the only way to teach math. After all, we reasoned, math is logical and sequential, and therefore a textbook is a necessity. I'm not sure I wholeheartedly agree with that any more -- but I will admit to struggling with a good way to teach math even now. Over the years, we've used mostly used textbooks/workbooks from *Miquon, Saxon*,[91] and *Math U See*.

None are without problems. All three have their pluses and minuses. I'm still searching for a good Math "non-textbook".[92] The closest I've found are *Calculadders*, which are designed to be used as a supplement to another "curriculum", not as a replacement. They are very well done worksheets for various levels and concepts, from beginning math through junior high level.

Out of a lack of time and energy to seek elsewhere, or start from scratch at this point, we will continue to use some sort of a math curriculum/textbook for now.

For younger students we were very happy with *Miquon* and Cuisenaire rods. The downside was that this is very teacher-involved and it only goes to about third or fourth grade. *Saxon* was okay for some of my students, including the current college math major. Enough said. I have many friends who use and love *Math U See*. We're using it for the first time this year – so I won't comment much on it yet.

---

[91] One of the biggest with *Saxon* is the lack of a separate Geometry course. They will tell you it is not a deficiency. But it is! (Actually, in the summer of 2009, Saxon finally came out with a Geometry textbook.)
[92] Perhaps I'll write one some day. Perhaps.

Four points I would like to make about Math before I move on:

1) I've come full circle on memorizing math facts – now I *strongly* believe we should get it out of the way fairly early (relatively speaking), because it needs to be done! Waiting too long only prolongs the agony!

2) My fourth child is majoring in math at college and doing very well – his formal homeschool math consisted of a few of the *Miquon* workbooks in his younger years and most of four *Saxon* textbooks (he never completed one!) in High School – so there is hope even when we are inconsistent in our approach to math.

3) Both logic and thinking skills are often underappreciated as important in math. But, I firmly believe that our family's focus on these has more than made up for our general lax attitude towards Math! When our Math curriculums have been shelved from time to time, we've still worked on Logic and Thinking Skills, often through *Building Thinking Skills* books and *Mathematical Reasoning* books.

4) Not all students, including those who are homeschooled, will excel in math. They all need to know how to balance their checkbooks, and keep a budget,

how to do basic addition, subtraction, multiplication, and division. And they should be comfortable with fractions – so that adjusting recipes does not cause frustration. Some mental math ability and the ability to approximate will serve them well in every day circumstances. But how much math do the rest of us truly use consistently?

The student who is not going to be a "math whiz" – can get some necessary math credits in courses other than Algebra 2 and Advanced Math. Why not Logic and History of Mathematics, for instance? I do think that Geometry is a good subject for most students, including those who don't like math in general. Geometry is more visual and consequently easier to grasp for many. We've moved Geometry above Algebra in our math "curriculum" – especially for those students who are "math-phobic".

Good Math Games & Manipulatives
- *Yahtzee*
- Cards
- Pattern Blocks
- *24 game*
- Dominos

Good Logic/Thinking Games
- Attribute Blocks
- Cards
- Stratego
- Set
- Mancala/Go/Othello type of games
- Chess

Other Math Resources
- *Mathematicians Are People, Too, 1 & 2*
- Money
- 100's Charts
- Cuisenaire Rods
- Clocks

Conclusion
Reading, writing, and arithmetic do need to have an important part in our home school. But they do not need to frustrate teachers or students! We need to be sure that we are not setting our standards or expectations because of what someone else expects.

Beyond reading, writing, and arithmetic, the Amish learn 3 additional R's in their homes: "Religion, respect, and responsibility".[93] We would do well to make these as important in our home education programs as "the 3 R's!"

---
[93] Charlotte Mason Companion, pg 30

FAMILY CIRCUS DAD IN THE CARTOON, "DO YOU REALIZE HOW RICH WE'D BE IF WE DIDN'T HAVE FOUR CHILDREN AND THREE PETS?" MOM'S RESPONSE: "NO, I REALIZE HOW POOR WE'D BE."[94]

Saving Money While Homeschooling

I have homeschooled many students on a shoestring budget for many years. It can be done! It's nice when money is available for "educational extras", but I try not to stress out when it's not. God does provide for our needs, but not always our wants! Over the two decades we have been at this adventure, here are a couple of the money saving methods I have discovered:

Make do with less – do you have to have it all? If you're using textbooks – do you really need one for each subject for each student? Will you really get your money's worth out of each of those Teachers' Guides and Answer Keys? (There are few times when I answer that question in the affirmative, but one is for higher level *Building Thinking Skills* and math books! I can figure those answers out when I have to, but I'd really rather not have to spend the time.) As I explained in the

---

[94] *Count Your Blessings* by Bill Keane – pg 37

Indispensable Chapter, we can save money by only purchasing the things that are highest priority on our lists.

Use the Internet
Over the years, I have also grown to appreciate the value of the internet more and more. For a recent 10-week class on Leonardo da Vinci, I bought about a dozen books to use in my research – and probably read over 100 websites. When I was researching astronomers for my "History of Astronomy" classes, almost all of my research was done on the web. Of course, I quickly found that not all websites were accurate in the information they presented – but then, neither are all books! For saving money (and time) the internet is hard to beat!

{And now, more than ever, purchasing e-books on the internet has become a real money saver!}

While saving money is important and very possible, don't do it unethically. Remember, someone took the time to develop the materials that you're considering. Don't copy what someone else has bought. Don't copy something and then return it as "new". And remember, sometimes even when you can make copies legally – your *time* may be worth more than the expense of an extra book.

In Conclusion
If your budget is not tight, rejoice. And still ensure that you are a good steward of the blessings God has given you. If your budget is tight, don't despair. Home education does not need to break the bank. There are very few things you have to have in order to teach your children at home. And there are many ways to spend less. Start thinking early about next year's topics of study – and then keep your eye out at used book sales, library sales, and yard sales. You'll be amazed at what you can find.

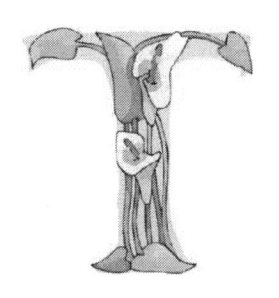

> "AS THEY MATURE WE ARE REAPING THE WONDERFUL BENEFITS WE ONLY DARED TO HOPE FOR – CHILDREN WHO ARE INTELLIGENT, SELF-DISCIPLINED, OBEDIENT, KIND, AND RESPONSIBLE (AT LEAST MOST OF THE TIME)."[95]

Teaching Teens

Does the above quote seem overly optimistic? I think it sums up what we all desire – and what we can all obtain "at least most of the time".

It's a shame that so many homeschoolers fear the teenage years. Every age brings unique challenges and unique pleasures. But there is something really special about the teenage years. The "difficult" tasks (like potty training, learning to read, etc.) are done by then.[96] Teens can generally listen well, read well, and argue well.[97] I thoroughly enjoy teaching classes with teenagers (which is why I was recently teaching three different high school classes a week and

---

[95] *Simplicity of Homeschooling*, pg 14
[96] Okay – teaching them to drive is not a piece of cake either. But we've survived that six times now, so I guess we'll manage with the next six.
[97] Call it "discuss well" if it makes you feel better, but with teens the two are basically synonymous.

coaching a Mock Trial team).[98] Teenagers in addition to our own are constantly coming and going at our house.

Why are home schoolers so often intimidated by the thought of teaching their teens? The answers I usually hear include:

- Concern over classes (especially "difficult" ones like foreign languages and higher math)
- Concern over credits and transcripts
- Concern about graduation
- Concern about getting into college

We'll look at each of these briefly, but let me first put these concerns in perspective:

What is the end we have in mind? Our family just celebrated the graduation of our fifth student. It was an exciting time. It was a joyous time. He had made it to the end of his studies under us. My responsibilities for his education had come to an end.

But was that night, the graduation ceremony, or even the official ending of his school work, the end that we had worked so hard to reach during all those years of teaching him at home?

Our first College Graduate with his youngest sister.

---

[98] [This past fall I taught four different high school classes and coached two mock trial teams.]

At one time, many years ago, we might have thought that that was the goal we were working to achieve. When we started on this road with our eldest child, 20+ years ago, that was undoubtedly the target we were shooting for. But slowly, over the years, our aim shifted. We realized that graduation was only part of the picture – we're preparing our children for life, not one event. Realizing that can help us enjoy the day-to-day effort and energy required.[99]

As I mentioned before, I think these are the types of things that should be high priority for us as we teach all of our students, especially our teens:
- Do they know and love God?
- Do they know and love God's word?
- Do they know how to research?
- Do they know how to debate?
- Do they know how to think?
- Do they know how to work?
- Do they know how to communicate?

Additionally, are our teens:
- Comfortable talking to adults? To their peers? To younger kids?
- Can they work independently? And in a group setting?
- Are they reading comfortably? And for enjoyment?
- Can they type? And use the computer?
- Can they find their way around the kitchen? Do laundry?

---

[99] Or, on bad days, to at least tolerate it!

- Do we have a vision for them? (God's vision, not ours)
- Do we recognize their strengths and weaknesses? Do they?
- Do we understand that we want them to develop wisdom <u>and</u> knowledge!
- How do we get our students where they're going? Let's look at these specific concerns now:

High School Classes
Considering home schooling through high school causes unnecessary stress in many families. How to handle higher level math classes and science labs and foreign languages rank at the head of most lists of potential problems. But why? It shouldn't be, for several reasons:

1) First of all, most homeschooling moms can personally handle teaching more of those classes than they give themselves credit for.

2) High schoolers can handle much more of the load themselves than we give them credit for – as I mentioned in a previous section on Math – my fourth child is currently a college math major. I didn't teach him upper level math – he taught it to himself. Now, remember, though, even when they can be self-taught, they are not necessarily self-motivated!

3) In many areas homeschooling mothers and fathers are offering many of these subjects as classes nowadays. In our area, I personally know of ongoing high school classes for home schoolers in Geometry, Physics, Chemistry, Biology, Astronomy, U.S. Constitution, French, Shakespeare, and English

Composition. And that's just among people I personally know.[100]

4) Correspondence schools are another option that we've tried for taking care of high school classes. It wasn't one of our favorites – but it did work. We've personally used the American School and CLASS. For some families it may be just the answer to these concerns.

I share those to show once again that our personal limitations are not our children's limitations, even when we teach them at home! Remember, home education = <u>parent-directed</u> education. Mom or Dad does not necessarily have to teach every subject to every child...So "difficult" high school classes should not cause insurmountable difficulties.

Additionally, most high school requirements are general in nature, not specific. For instance, our "church covering" does not require specific science credits such as Biology, Chemistry, and Physics (and neither do most colleges!). But, instead they require 4 credits of science of our choosing, and likewise 4 credits of English, 3 of math, and 4 social studies credits. Each family (or each student within a family) can pick the specific courses within each general subject that they

---

[100] [And since the first edition, that list has grown MUCH longer. There are very few subjects NOT being offered by homeschoolers for homeschoolers these days.]

want to take. And remember, these are the minimums, not the maximums! Most of my family tends to be light on the Math and Science but heavy on the English and Social Studies.[101]

Of course, there is no shortage of good electives they can take: Art, Music, Typing, Computer Science, Drivers' Training,[102] to name a few.

And as we direct their education, we can involve them in Community Theater, music programs, government clubs, and much more to round out their education – all of which counts towards their high school credits.

Credits and Transcripts
How to award credits for high school classes is a big, but mostly needless, concern. I know of two accepted standards for awarding a credit.

1) Starting and completing a high school level textbook.

2) Logging approximately 120 – 150 hours in a specific subject – reading, discussing, listening to lectures, writing about it, and watching related videos all count towards the necessary time. I found the book *Design-Form-U-La* to be very helpful when we started keeping these kinds of records.

---

[101] But I guess that comes from having a mother who thoroughly enjoys Shakespeare and History!!! (Not that I don't enjoy Math – I just have a harder time getting excited about teaching it!)
[102] If we were short credits, we would include Driver's Training on the transcript – but my students already have so many credits, we don't find it necessary to include it.

Our family grants most credits based on the "hours logged" in a subject, rather than through textbook completion, since we use so few textbooks, even in high school. Textbooks are not totally bad – but they are so two-dimensional! Learning can and should be three-dimensional.

High school (even at home) can include:
- Athletics
- Drama
- Essay/speech contests,

And they can generally receive high school credit for work done before high school, in seventh or eighth grade, if it's high school level work.

Transcripts also intimidate many folks – but they're really easy to do. The standard way is to break courses up by school year, one section for the freshman year, one for the sophomore year, etc…But we prefer to show them by subjects instead, with all the English classes listed together, and then the math, and then the science, etc. I've included a sample transcript in the appendix. Feel free to modify them it anyway that makes it useful for your family.

Transcripts need to include the student's name, date of birth, and school years covered. Each class listed should include the general subject it was in (such as science), followed by the specific Course title (such as Biology), a grade, and a credit (usually ½ or 1). Not too complicated. It's better if it's done on a computer, though it doesn't have to be!

Portfolios of high school work are nice too – we've never used them in any official way –but they're nice to show grandparents and other interested folks. Portfolios can include all sorts of things – essays they've written, programs from plays they've been in, music they've written, artwork, test scores, copies of transcripts and progress reports – the possibilities are endless.

Graduation

Graduation is an exciting time for students and parents alike – it is not the end of the journey, but merely acknowledgement of passing through into another stage. It can be commemorated by a simple party at home, or a larger ceremony in a church or other large facility, or merely a passing recognition of the fact. Of our first five home school high school graduates, three participated in ceremonies, and two "didn't bother". There is no right or wrong way to "graduate" a home educated student.

When my niece Melissa graduated, she participated in a big graduation ceremony with dozens of other students in our home school covering (like my 4th and 5th graduates had done), and then she had a graduation party. At her party, she gave out notes to her guests, with this scripture: "Wisdom is the principal thing; Therefore get wisdom. And in all your getting, get understanding."[103] And then she added, "My high school days have certainly been a journey in getting wisdom. Thank you for being a part of my journey. God has used you in my life, as He's brought me to a greater understanding of wisdom. I'm thankful for you, and I'm thankful for you being here today to help me celebrate the end of one part of my journey and the start of another. Thank you!"

---

[103] Proverbs 4:7

When Ariel, my fifth child, graduated, he requested the privilege of singing at his graduation ceremony. As the date came closer, he could not find a song he liked, so he wrote his own for the occasion. There were few dry eyes in the church that night when he sang his song of thanks, which included the following poignant words: "Thank you, for your love, for the memories, for the times we shared, I don't deserve you, but I'm glad you're here...Wherever I go, you're with me...Thank you, for your heart...For the dreams we dared. I don't deserve you, but I'm thankful you cared...Nothing lasts forever, but your love will last me a lifetime."

When it gets close to that time, plan a graduation event, big or small, that will bless your family, and meet the needs of your special student(s).

College
College is a big concern for parents of high schoolers, also. But it doesn't have to be.

1) Not all students should go on to college. (My desire is to prepare mine so that going is not a problem if and when God directs them down that path.)

2) If they do go, they can start while they're still in high school (and living at home!), right out of high

school, or even later on. Two of my oldest children have delayed college as they pursue other paths right now (like the mission field).

3) Good scores on standardized tests will make entrance into many colleges easier – but bad scores will not needlessly hinder the process! One of my oldest is very smart, but freezes up on tests. Consequently her test scores are not super high. But she was able to get into a local community college, where she did fine, and then she was able to transfer to a 4-year university.

4) More and more colleges are looking for home-educated applicants as they realize what good students they typically are, and how well most of them do in the college world.

5) Even if your teen doesn't take (m)any formal classes during high school, he should do fine in college classes, if he knows <u>how to study</u>. That is so much more important than the specific knowledge he has or has not gained. One of my students found in college that he had gaps in his World History knowledge, since we had focused on some specific periods to the exclusion of others. But he was able to fill those gaps quickly and easily as he took the college class. He had also never taken a Computer Science class before college, but he aced the first one he took, because he knew how to study, and how to apply himself.

6) And before we panic about how our high schoolers are doing, let's make sure our expectations are reasonable. The National Assessment of Educational Progress results showed in 1994[104] that among mostly public-schooled high schoolers – only 36% were reading at a "proficient" level in 12th grade. Only 36% of 11th graders were writing at a "proficient" level. Only 60% could do basic math – and only 7% could solve multi-step problems and beginning Algebra[105] And an entire book, *What Do Our 17-Year-Olds Know?* deals with how little most of them do know. ....What are **we** worried about?

Let's end this chapter with two concerns that I think parents do need to think about:

1) Teenage boys are quickly becoming men. That means they need interaction with other teenage boys and with adult men, not just younger siblings and with mom. They cannot just answer to Mom. While obedience is necessary – they are quickly growing beyond what we alone can give them. Moms, DON'T take it personally if your teenage son is pulling away from you. It's natural and it's necessary. He is becoming a man!

2) One of the growing trends among homeschoolers {at least in the States} has been to rush their kids through their schooling and graduate them early. Our third child graduated when she was 16, mostly so that she could start dancing with a professional ballet company. Our fourth and fifth, could have both

---

[104] And I'm sure the trend has gotten worse – not better!
[105] From a publication called "Reaching the Next Step" -- put out by the AFT Educational Issues Department in Washington, D.C.

graduated at least a year early. But for both of them, there was the realization that they would give up more than they would gain if they shortened their high school years. And now that we've been at this for 20 plus years, I am more convinced that what they realized is true in more cases than not. Why do we want to be in such a big hurry to graduate our students? They certainly aren't lacking for subjects that they can study at home. What do we gain and what do they gain by rushing the process, versus what is lost – more time with their family; more time to mature; more time to pursue special interests? There are exceptions, of course, but I think home schoolers would do well to rethink this trend.

Conclusion

I hope I have encouraged you with this chapter. Please prayerfully consider teaching your teens and enjoying them in the process!!! And on a positive note, may we all live to see the day that our children "rise up and call us blessed". A couple of years back one of my older sons sent me a very special email. In his email, he reworked much of Proverbs 31 for me. Among other things, it included these special words:

"Dad has found an excellent wife. Your worth is far above jewels...You get good deals through the coop...You extend your hand to friends who are lacking...All your household are clothed with scarlet (and everything else they need) ...You a very wise woman...Bless you Mom." When I am having rough day, and I have my share of those, his words, and similar words from his siblings, are a great comfort to me. He ended that email with: *"I love you mom, and appreciate everything that you have done. You are a great mother, and you're doing a great job!!! Be blessed!!!"* How can a Mom not be blessed by those words?!?

> "IT IS A VERY GRAVE MISTAKE TO THINK THAT THE ENJOYMENT OF SEEING AND SEARCHING CAN BE PROMOTED BY MEANS OF COERCION AND A SENSE OF DUTY."
> ALBERT EINSTEIN

Unit Studies / Topical Studies

If you've already tried "Unit Studies" and have been turned off by them, please read this chapter anyway. I may be able to give you a new perspective on what "Unit Studies" can do for your family.

After 20 years of homeschooling, I have to say: I am excited about learning! I am excited about "school"! And so are my kids! It's not that my kids are perfect, or that we don't have bad days. But all in all, at our house, learning is something to get excited about.

Do some of you struggle with reluctant students? Do some of you struggle with "lazy" students? Are you having trouble hanging in there until the end of the year? Maybe it's time you reevaluate your methods, rather than giving in and giving up.

First, a couple more definitions are in order. "Unit studies" typically mean specific studies revolving around a *particular topic, but covering multiple subjects*. A KONOS unit on character, for instance, may include history, science, English, etc. Most unit studies do not try to incorporate math, but typically they'll at least touch on most other subjects.

A friend and I coined the term "topical study" a few years back, to describe something more limited in nature, a study of a *particular topic within a subject*. For instance, we study history topically – the Civil War might be our topic for a year, and the Lewis and Clark Expedition would be our topic a different time. These topical studies may cover some other subjects as well, art or music, or science, for instance, but they are primarily dealing with a particular topic.

We've been homeschooling for so long that we've gone full circle with methods several times. We have used KONOS, straight textbooks alone and with a correspondence school, unschooling, relaxed schooling, our own unit studies, topical studies, and classes with other homeschoolers. There are advantages and disadvantages to the various methods, but my family continues to go back to unit studies and topical studies!

Real learning involves getting familiar with something and getting comfortable with it! Familiarity and comfort don't come when one topic after another is thrown at a learner. They come from repetition and context.

We must encounter the same words, the same concepts, the same dates many times before we "own" them, before they become a part of our vocabulary, something that we remember. Textbook teaching does not lead to this kind of ownership very often.

In my humble opinion (my bias will definitely show here) History and Science should be taught exclusively with the Topical Study/Unit Study method through at least eighth grade (and sometimes even in high school). Is it too painfully obvious here that I have an aversion to textbooks? It's not that textbooks are totally worthless, but close. Let's be honest here: How often do you go to a textbook to find the answer to a question? How much of what you endured "learning" through textbooks, do you actually remember? Enough said.

John Holt (a well-known unschooler back in the days when we began our homeschooling journey) talked about "how children fail" and "how children learn". He suggested that if we have reluctant and/or lazy students, we should blame our materials and/or our methods, not our students! And please remember that most of us are basing our methods and materials on the public school systems – because that's the only thing we know. As John Gatto reminds us in *Dumbing Us Down*, the public school system is failing, so why are we trying so hard to copy it?

Many years ago, Gregg Harris proposed "delight directed studies" to take care of the perceived problem of a reluctant and/or lazy student. This can be our delight or their delight. This is a very important point when you start looking at Unit Studies. You need to pick something your family will get excited about.

One of the questions often voiced about using unit studies is, "What if I miss something this way, what if I don't cover something that should have been covered?" My first response when someone asks that question is, "Covered according to whom?" Contrary to what some folks would lead us to believe there is no one "correct" curriculum for, say, fourth grade, or sixth grade, or any other grade. Look at the charts I've made comparing different curriculums in the *Multi-level Teaching* and *Nature and Science* chapters; the different curriculums usually have less in common with each other rather than more.

Next, remember that covering material does not equal learning it! There is an important distinction here! Please don't miss it. With topical/unit studies, we *cover* less, and *learn* more.

Also, with multiple students in family topical studies actually simplify things for mom. The year I knew we had to do something different was the year we had three students and we were using three different history books. I was trying to keep up with three students in three very different books, covering three very different topics! And that was just in the one subject!

Now I realize that for many of you, "multiple students" won't have the same impact on the number of different books you would be using as it did for me. I maxed out at seven students in one school year, and I should have five or six each year for the next eight years or so, then it might start tapering down. But even if you only have two students it can still make a difference!

Topical studies also give siblings something in common: shared knowledge and experiences. We can carry our "school" discussions much beyond the "classroom" this way, since several of us are studying the same thing at the same time. And that includes me, since I am spending my time preparing a topical study, instead of writing out lesson plans, grading tests, and checking assignments.

One of the additional beauties of a topical study/unit study is the ability to study two or more subjects at the same time (=efficiency). Unit Studies are typically geared to hit multiple subjects at the same time. While Topical Studies are generally more limited in focus, they can still incorporate multiple subjects.

For instance, we recently combined art and science when we did leaf rubbings at a local park. The mom who organized the outing is quite knowledgeable about trees, so while the kids (and I) were making pictures, she explained what kind of tree each was from, and shared various other tidbits about the trees at the same time.

Another good combination is English and History. Biographies and historical fiction cover both well, and poetry related to history is also a good way to combine the two. These types of studies are more relevant and more efficient than trying to cover each "subject" separately!

Why do we want to go to the "trouble" of unit studies? It is more trouble than just picking up a textbook and going through it. But it is also more effective! It's more fun! And it's usually more enjoyable for students and teacher alike!

I hope you're convinced, and that you want to try unit/topical studies. Now what??? How do you actually plan the studies?

There are lots and lots of published studies out there now (a big change from when I started over 20 years ago!) And no, I haven't tried them all, but I've tried several: *KONOS, Considering God' Creation, Prepare & Pray*, to name a few. These are great starting points, but be sure to adapt even these to your own family! They are each a tool, a guide, not a task master.

Ultimately, you should really try your own topical studies. They don't have to be long. (Even though ours usually end up being long!) You might want to start with something small, like a 2 week study. They don't have to be involved. And you don't have to pull them from thin air. A good place to begin is with a topic someone is really interested in. That's how ours usually begin. The key to successful topical studies is often *timing* and *interest*!

Some good science topics to begin with: (But remember, "the sky's the limit"!)
- Birds
- Bugs
- Butterflies
- Seven Days of Creation
- Creation vs. Evolution (we want our children to be critical thinkers!)
- Gardening
- Animal Husbandry
- Flowers
- Dinosaurs

Biblical/Christian topics:
- Martyrs
- Missionaries

Some good history topics:
- U.S. Presidents (1/week, for instance)

- British Kings and Queens
- Leonardo da Vinci

Specific Wars
- Revolutionary War
- Civil War
- World War II

Specific Eras
- Renaissance
- Reformation
- Middle Ages – knights, castles…

Geography studies
- U.S. States (all 50 – 1 per week, for example)
- Countries (within a continent)
- Continent (1/month)

Anything else of interest to your family!!!

Once you have a topic, where do you begin?
- The library
- Your own books
- Encyclopedias
- On-line research
- Used books
- Friends
- Experts

I find that once I've chosen a topic — the resources practically jump out at me.

Start with a schedule/timeline for your study. Do you want to study the topic for two weeks or two months? Have a starting schedule, but be flexible...If it fizzles out sooner, stop! If you're having so much fun, you want to continue when your time is up, continue!

One main topic/day works well for us; we incorporate:
- "Lectures" (one of my favorites)
- Read alouds (a favorite for most of the students!)
- Silent reading assignments
- Research Assignments (give written or oral reports)
- Art assignments (could include drawing/collages/sculpture)

[106]

With topical studies you can cover U.S. or World History in depth, over years. Why "cover it all" in one year, again and again, never really going into any detail?

In Conclusion
If you haven't tried topical studies or unit studies with your family, please do. If you have and didn't like it, please try it again. Your family could benefit greatly from the experience!

---

[106] So maybe their drawings won't look like Leonardo da Vinci's — but even he had to start somewhere.

"THERE AND BACK AGAIN...."[107]

Vacations

Traveling is my idea of a family vacation. The only overseas travel we have done as a family was in conjunction with a military assignment, but I wouldn't trade those opportunities for anything.[108]

I like family vacations – short ones, long ones, it doesn't matter. I like to be together as a family, away from home, away from the distractions of the phones, and the never ending housework, and the electronic devises that permeate our lives. (I first wrote that paragraph two years ago, and how quickly things change – now we just take most of that with us. On our last family trip, we had three cell phones, one lap top computer, and two pocket PC's with us! So much for leaving electronic distractions at home!)[109]

We don't take big, fancy, expensive vacations, mind you. A vacation for us is anything we do away from home for a few

---

[107] Bilbo in *The Hobbit*
[108] [Subsets of the family have made MANY trips overseas at this point – including the numerous mission trips mentioned in the Questions and Answers chapter, and a trip to Panama that my husband and I made a couple of years ago.]
[109] [Of course – that trip was many years ago – this list would pale by comparison to today's list of electronic devices that accompany us on most trips these days!]

days or more. It's often in conjunction with a move or work, but occasionally it's just for fun. One of our biggest vacation trip was when Dan retired from the military a few years back. We spent 20 days on the road in the western United States. We pulled a borrowed tent trailer behind our big van and camped most of the trip. It was great. Of course, it was also exhausting; by time we neared the end of the trip, my kids had decided we should skip *the Grand Canyon*, rather than have to set up and sleep in the tent trailer one more night!

I **don't** particularly like the work involved in preparing for a trip – the planning, purchasing, and packing that all have to happen before we can even get out the door. I have to keep reminding myself that it will all be worth it once we get on our way. (Our last trip started off better than most – my 23-year-old son did most of the advance preparations! What a treat!) But once we leave the house behind, I generally know it's all worth it.

I like trips for many reasons – the historical places we visit – the National Parks, the Zoos, even an occasional museum. We also get to visit with extended family and old and new friends on many of our trips. (Yes, we even have friends who can find enough floor space for all of us!) In fact, we usually camp or stay with friends and only rarely stay in motels, thus keeping down costs.

We usually plan our trips based on where we're heading, how much time we can spend getting there, and which wonderful places along the way we can fit in. My children could not begin to tell you of all the castles they visited in Germany, or all the Civil War and Revolutionary War sites they've visited up and down the east coast.

Trips are such a wonderful way to have fun and learn as a family. We like to listen to tapes/CD's while we're traveling. Audio has a lot of advantages over video – for many reasons – portability being the first one! But the primary one is that it enables the listeners to use their imagination to follow the story, instead of having all the work done for them. Much like having a good book read aloud. (Which we've also done on trips.)

Our family favorites include:
- *Hank the Cowdog*[110] (not necessarily educational, but entertaining!)
- *Focus on the Family's Odyssey*[111] (entertaining and often educational)
- *Focus on the Family's Chronicles of Narnia* (wonderful!)
- *Jonathan Park*[112] (our newest favorite – combining Creation Science with fun stories)

And portable games are a great way to use traveling time (board games, word games, and card games).

We also use some of our driving time to prepare for the sites we're going to visit; I'm usually reading the books/information I've brought along as we drive, and then sharing the information with the rest of the family.

---

[110] Published by Maverick Books – for more information, see the official website: http://www.hankthecowdog.com/
[111] Published by Focus on the Family – for more information, see http://www.family.org/
[112] For more information, see their website: www.JonathanPark.com .

In addition to what we take with us, any big trips also involve the purchase of souvenirs. To keep that from getting out of hand, we usually give each of the kids a small budget for their own souvenirs, typically a set amount for each day of the trip. That way they can decide whether they want a bunch of small things, or something bigger like a t-shirt. Souvenirs, photos and memories are all part of the fun of traveling.

Letterboxing[113]

Recently we were introduced by friends to letterboxing, which reminds me of a cross between a scavenger hunt and the volksmarching we used to love in Germany. We have only been adding letterboxing to trips for the last six months – but we've already had some great times with it, and look forward to finding many, many more letterboxes!

Letterboxing in Sewanee, TN.

Summary

If you don't already take family vacations – please consider it. Vacations don't have to be expensive and they don't have to be stressful. They should be together and fun. It's not time "off of school", it's just education with another dimension. Remember to record all the neat educational things your kids do when traveling.

---

[113] For more information, see www.atlasquest.com .

> "LESSON PLANS COME BEFORE – PROGRESS REPORTS COME AFTER. WANT TO GUESS WHICH I DEEM MORE IMPORTANT?"
> ~~CATHY JAIME (ME!) IN A WORKSHOP

Writing it all up
(Lesson plans, Record keeping, etc.)

Record Keeping – something most of us fear to some degree or another. For the purpose of this chapter, we will discuss records made beforehand (study and lesson plans) and then records made afterwards (progress reports and transcripts).

The length and the depth of both kinds can vary significantly, depending on family preferences and {legal} requirements.

Mary Hood's book, *Relaxed Record Keeping,* was very helpful to me when we moved to Alabama, and I had to get more serious about our formal records. And *Design Form-U-La* by Barb Shelton was encouraging when I started getting more creative with teaching teens and needed ideas for that record keeping. I heartily recommend both of them to anyone who needs more help in this area.

Lesson Plans
We write lesson plans to give an overview of what we plan to cover in our upcoming subject(s). This can be as simple as a textbook table of contents, with a notation on pages or chapters to cover each week. They can also be more detailed,

particularly in the case of topical studies, where books will be noted, and projects listed, etc.

These plans are a good idea –as long as it is understood that they are just that – <u>plans</u>. (Our home school covering calls this a Study Plan, and requires that it be done before each school year.) Plans should always be <u>flexible</u>. Allowance needs to be made in case of illness, unexpected company or vacation, or even an unplanned educational opportunity. (We should question our priorities when we're too busy doing "school" to do something educational. Not to say that we need to chase after every educational opportunity – we might never be home!) Again, there needs to be a balance.

Progress Reports (or Report Cards)
These are one way to report how students have done in their course work. We do them twice during every school year as required – January and June – though of course a family could do them more often if they desired.

Our family prefers to use grades as little as possible – since they are an extremely subjective device. We only use a simple pass/fail designation for the coursework of our younger students. Of course, as with all other decisions, this one must be made by each family for itself.

High School Transcripts
I've included information on transcripts in the *Teaching Teens* chapter. There is also a sample of the way we make transcripts in the Appendix.

Final Thoughts
Our records are important – but they should be because they're important to us – not because they are important to someone else. They do not need to be complicated, and they do not need to be overwhelming.

> "FOR UNTO US A CHILD IS BORN, UNTO US A SON IS GIVEN; AND THE GOVERNMENT WILL BE UPON HIS SHOULDER. AND HIS NAME WILL BE CALLED WONDERFUL, COUNSELOR, MIGHTY GOD, EVERLASTING FATHER, PRINCE OF PEACE." ISAIAH 9:6

X-mas[114] and Other Holidays

Holy Days were set apart by the Lord for His people to remember, to remember Him, and to remember His grace and mercy to His people. Have we lost "holy days" today?

Holidays bring our families closer together, build memories, and help enforce historical religious events. The secular world works hard to take God out of Thanksgiving and Christ out of Christmas – let's work hard to keep Him where He belongs.

---

[114] X is from the Greek word for Christ; X-mas has been used as an accepted substitution for Christmas for centuries, and is not meant here in an offensive manner!

I understand that not all Christians celebrate Christmas. But our family has made the choice to celebrate it. Starting the fourth Sunday before Christmas, we begin celebrating Advent[115] – this is such a good time to reflect on the prophesies of Christ's birth, on the events surrounding His birth, and the reasons for it. (Our need of a Savior – Christmas points us to the Cross and the Resurrection!) We enjoy our favorite Christmas hymns, many of which contain the gospel message.

And we enjoy simple family traditions and family togetherness. We do exchange gifts – but we've managed to keep that low key – having started our family on a tight budget 26 years ago helps, I'm sure. The fun is more in the giving than in the receiving. Each child has a small budget with which to purchase gifts for their family members, and they anxiously await the giving of those gifts on Christmas – much more than anticipating what they will receive.

---

[115] Advent looks forward to the "coming of Christ". It is typically celebrated the 4 Sundays prior to Christmas with an Advent Wreath and 4 candles. An additional candle is lit each week – usually along with some scriptures, songs, and treats. Some groups consider the 4 candles to stand for: Hope, Peace, Joy, and Love; while others consider them to stand for The Prophets, Angels, Shepherds, and Magi. An additional candle in the midst of the wreath represents Christ, and is generally lit on either Christmas Eve or Christmas Day. We learned about and embraced the tradition while living in Germany many years ago.

God gave us the greatest gift on Christmas – and the wise men honored Him with their gifts on Epiphany – celebrating Christ as Prophet, Priest, and King. May we honor Him and each other with our gifts of love and appreciation and service.

Each family must determine its own convictions on a day like Halloween. I certainly do not want to give Satan any extra mileage on that day. In some cases it can be an opportunity to share the gospel (tracts with trick or treat candy), but again each family must decide what works for it. As a Protestant I would rather emphasis Reformation Day on October 31st. That was the day Martin Luther chose to post his 95 thesis on the church door. We have had Reformation Day Celebrations many years on that day – and I believe that puts our focus back on the Lord, where it belongs.

A group of holidays we Christians tend to overlook are the Jewish holidays that are part of our spiritual heritage. What a shame that we so seldom include Passover, Hanukah, and the others in our celebrations. May more of us be motivated to include these in our "curriculum". A great book to get lots of ideas for this is *A Family Guide to the Biblical Holidays* by Robin Scarlata and Linda Pierce.

In Conclusion

May we all get to the point where we can embrace the holidays as Holy Days to recall God and His Providence. They are not just interruptions to our schedules, or excuses to watch football.[116] Can we say with Bilbo in *Fellowship of the Ring*, "I need a holiday, a very long holiday"? Holidays can and should be an important part of our lives and our "curriculum".

---

[116] Not that we don't watch football in our home!

Y

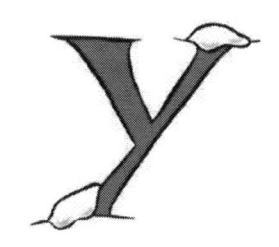

"JESUS CHRIST IS THE SAME YESTERDAY, TODAY, AND FOREVER."
HEBREWS 13:8

Yesterday, Today, and Tomorrow (w/Homeschooling)

Yesterday

When we began homeschooling our children over 20 years ago, it was like treading on an unmarked path {at least in the United States}. Yes, others had homeschooled before us. But the numbers were few, the resources available were few, and the support was so much less than today. But we did it. Because we believed it was the best thing for our children. And most importantly we did it because God wanted us to. We wouldn't change those early years for the world.

People ask us many times why we began to teach our children at home. My husband Dan and I had both been public schooled. We both went to M.I.T., a top engineering school in Massachusetts. We both believe, when all was said and done, that we got into M.I.T. <u>in spite</u> of our formal educations, not because of them! Even before our first child was born, we were both reading books on educational options, because we both believed there had to be something better than the paths we had taken through school.

By the time our first child was kindergarten age, we knew she belonged at home. We knew we wanted more for her than we had received in the state-run school system. And we worked to give her that.

The home schooling "movement" has come along a long ways in the 30+ years since my family started on this journey. At that time, support groups mostly existed only in the planning stages, or in the minds of forward-looking parents. Books on the subject were few. And curriculum choices were fairly limited as well.

When support groups didn't exist, we helped start them. When we lived overseas, away from the early Curriculum Fairs, we hosted our own. And when "homeschooling" material was scare – we looked elsewhere.[117] Worthwhile material was out there – we just had to work harder to find it!

Today
Today, most of that has changed significantly {again, at least in the U.S.}. Currently, it is legal to teach our own children in all 50 states. Support groups exist across the country, and in many communities the difficulty is in choosing *which one* to join! Choosing from the many home school materials available now can be a mind boggling affair.

Tomorrow
What can we say about tomorrow? Only God knows what tomorrow holds, but we can certainly look forward, knowing that He holds it in His hands. We can also continue to pray for our rights as parents. As I work to finish this book, at least two states have begun actively harassing homeschoolers, and several other states are considering revising their laws, generally against homeschoolers. This should not cause us to worry, but it should cause us to stay alert!

---

[117] In my early years as a homeschoolers, I subscribed to two "regular" teacher magazines and belong to two "regular" teacher book clubs.

> "SO GOD CREATED GREAT SEA CREATURES AND EVERY LIVING THING THAT MOVES, WITH WHICH THE WATERS ABOUNDED, ACCORDING TO ITS KIND. AND GOD SAW THAT IT WAS GOOD."
> GENESIS 1:21

Zoos, Museums, Other Memberships

Many of our favorite educational experiences have included educational places where we've had memberships. Family memberships can lead to such wonderful, inexpensive, educational, multi-level, multi-subject experiences. If you are doubting the inexpensive part, please keep reading. (Of course, this is one of the few places that small families are actually at a disadvantage, but they can still benefit from these.)

In Germany, we had a membership for six months at a "Garden Show". It travels from place to place in Germany every two years, and came to our beautiful city during our stay there. We talked another homeschooling family into also spending the $60 that a family membership cost, and we each probably went more than 20 times in the six months. We learned about flowers, birds, American Indians,[118] music, crafts, and so much more. The bulk of our schooling during those six months for many different ages tied into something we did at the Garden Show. Where else could we have gotten such a return on our educational investment?

In the five years since we've been in Alabama we've had the following memberships at various times: U.S. Space & Rocket Center; Constitution Hall Village; Huntsville Art Museum; Nashville Zoo; Birmingham Zoo; Tennessee Aquarium; Creative Discovery Museum; Berman Museum; and Natural History Museum in Anniston. We obviously like day trips. For me, anything within a 100 mile range is fair game for a good day trip. And we are fortunate to be right at or under 100 miles from Nashville, Chattanooga, Birmingham, and Anniston. Talk about great opportunities!

Sometimes we'll invite others to join us, but more often, it's just our family. We pack a cooler with drinks and sandwich fixings, grab a couple of boxes of cheap crackers and/or cookies, and we're almost ready to go out the door. Of course there's also the camera, and clipboards, too! When we're in the mood to do this frequently, we have clipboards, tote bags, and colored pencils (we don't "do" crayons!) ready for each child to grab as we head out the door.

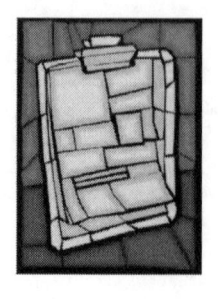

---

[118] Visiting from a sister city in New York.

And "Odysseys" or other audios for the drive. Remember, "getting there is half the fun!" We make this type of trip as often as weekly, or as seldom as every month or so, depending on what else is going on in our lives. It's a great way to make learning three-dimensional!

Visits can be tied into home research, books from the library, and so much more. They can be turned into a full-blown "unit study" or they can just be a short term "topical" study.

In conjunction with this, remember, field trips are fun, field trips are generally interesting, and yes, field trips are school. Please don't let anyone tell you otherwise. Some advance preparation and follow up after will strengthen the value of the field trip. On the other hand, don't feel obligated to go on trips just because someone else suggests it. They have to fit in with your lifestyles and your goals. For our family, sending <u>some</u> of the kids on a field trip is often a good option when it's not appropriate for everyone. I try not to be jealous when my children get to do more neat things than I do!

Summary
I would strongly encourage you to look into a family membership somewhere close by, if you don't already have at least one! Many of them are especially good deals because

they are reciprocal – you can use them at other museums or zoos. We visited museums for *free* in Chicago and Boston, because we joined an Alabama science museum last summer. What a bargain!

[And if they are still outside of your budget – you can drop hints for them for gifts! My sister gave me a membership to the Aquarium one year, it was a wonderful gift! And many people I know get memberships from the grandparents to various museums, zoos, etc. Definitely gifts that will give all year!]

Conclusion

I hope you have been encouraged as I've shared some of our family's experiences on our home education journey. I pray that this "alphabet book for grown-ups" has successfully entertained and educated you on the many options available in this wide world of education.

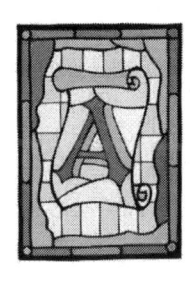

A to *Z*

All of us who are home educating, or considering doing so, have at least one *critical* thing in common – we want what's best for our children! Because of that, *we* want to be the ones to direct their education. As I've tried to share with you – education can take many forms. Ultimately we will each choose the direction that's best for our own family, as we prayerfully lay our students before the Lord.

May God bless you greatly in your educational endeavors – whether you have 1 student, or 12 students, or any other number!

Don't fret about mistakes and be sure to celebrate the successes!

I want to end this book with some very encouraging words -- encouraging words one of my own children sent me in the form of a 10-page letter of thanks several years ago. I received the letter the day I was speaking at a Moms' Meeting on "Teaching Teens". That night as I shared portions of this letter with the group it brought tears to many eyes. It began:

> *"I wanted to write and thank you for the things you have done for me in my life. God has been teaching me much the past two months, and a realization of my ungratefulness is among the many things He has shown me. Wow! Please forgive me for the lifestyle of ungratefulness which I have lived. I'm sorry. I was wrong."* (She went on to thank me for so many things that tied directly to this book that I just have to share them. I have changed her order, to match the order of the chapters of the book – but the words are all hers!):

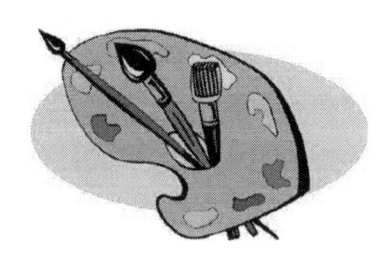

ART: *"Thank you for the exciting drawing videos and books that opened my imagination and revealed the gift God gave me." "Thank you for encouraging me to enter writing contests, and art contests, for the purpose of stretching my skills." "Thank you for all the times you traveled nearly an hour away to various cities for the homeschool art classes."*

BIBLE: *"Thank you for taking me to church while I was still young, so that I could learn about God. Thank you for teaching me that God is Holy, and just." "Thank you for teaching me the importance of scripture memory at a young age."*

ENCYCLOPEDIAS and OTHER REFERENCES: *"Thank you for training me to search for answers — for all the times you sent me to dictionary when I didn't know how to spell a word, or understand the definition."*

HISTORY and GEOGRAPHY: *"Thank you for teaching me the importance of history -- because there truly is 'nothing new under the sun' and history does repeat itself. Thank you for all the awesome field trips to castles, and zoos, and even museums." "Thank you for constantly searching for new ways to make learning hands-on — like Tour Europe[119] and trips to Science museums." "Thank you that you took us orienteering in Kitzegen and Worms, etc. etc. I am shocked daily by how few people are truly comfortable reading maps. So thank you also for the times of allowing us to 'navigate' down the autobahns. Thank you for teaching me how to 'get around' by bus. (Again another skill I'm shocked that 'everyone' doesn't know.)"*

INDISPENSIBLE: *"Thank you for the ever-growing "world of books" library you opened up to us — to this day some of the most interesting/impacting books I've read came from browsing there at my leisure."*[120] *"Thank you for the 'Anne of Greene Gables' book series — they're one of my all-time favorites."*[121] *"Thank you for the awesome trips to the Library Bookstore."*

---

[119] For our support group's Geography Fair one year each family did a country in Europe.
[120] A family library is truly priceless!
[121] I had forgotten giving her that series! But she had not.

JUMPING JACKS: *"Thank you for enrolling me in physical activities and giving me creative outlets. Thank you for opening the world of dance to me by enrolling me in my first lessons."*

NATURE and OTHER SCIENCES: *"Thank you for not forcing me to take the Biology class. I would have hated it!"*[122]

OURSELVES OR WITH OTHERS: *"Thank you for being involved in local homeschool groups so that we learned to socialize. Thank you for the times you took positions of servant leadership in both large and small ways. I was proud of you!"*

PHILOSOPHY OF EDUCATION: *"Thank you for all the home-cooked meals, the home-made clothes, and especially the home-taught years. Thank you for loving me enough to home school me." "Thank you for making life my school instead of school becoming my life." "Thank you for teaching me that learning is a lifetime process and a LIVE thing, not merely memorizing facts out of an inaccurate secular-humanist textbook."*

---

[122] And I almost made her take that class, since she "needed" the lab work! I'm so glad I followed my instinct instead.

READING, WRITING, and ARITHMETIC: *"Thanks for teaching me an appreciation of fine literature." "For teaching me typing, layout, and general newsletter editing skills through hands-on experience – THANK YOU!" "Thank you for the adventurous lessons in consumer economics through flea markets and yard sales."*

TEACHING TEENS: *"Thank you for teaching me to take initiative, when I need or want to learn something." "Thank you for training me to cook, and to grocery shop, to do laundry, to conserve energy, to love "treasure hunting" (yard saling), to love reading." "Thank you for opening the world of 'clothes making' up to me by the basics of using a sewing machine." "Thank you for teaching me responsibility with chores and community service." "Thank you for the freedom to express my unique personality in the way I dressed growing up (even if others were embarrassed to be around me). Thank you for teaching me that there are more important things in life than the clothes brand I wear, or the toys I own." "Thank you for the bits of advice these past few years as I juggled the question of college, career, or 'what?'" "Thank you for teaching me 'how' to be on time – by planning to be early (even if I don't always apply it.)*

ZOOS, MUSEUMS, OTHER MEMBERSHIPS: *"Thank you for the GARDEN SHOW!!! Such awesome projects, and lessons we did. So many skills packed into the experience. WOW! What a privilege. Thank you for allowing us to create our own personal t-shirts."*[123]

---

[123] We attended the Garden Show regularly with another family that year, and all the kids in both families designed their own t-shirts to wear on our regular trips there.

Although they are highly personal, I share these words of thanks with you in the hopes that you will be encouraged as well – and that you will someday be blessed by your children in similar ways.

I hope my daughter's words of gratitude have blessed you, and that this book has blessed you. Our family is not perfect, our homeschooling is not perfect. But we serve a perfect God. And He can use all that we do – when we turn it over to Him – for His glory and good. Well, actually, He uses *all* of it for His glory and good – whether we turn it over to Him or not. Doing so increases *our* blessings and enjoyment!

May your home education experience be truly blessed by Him.

Yours in Christ,

Cathy

Bibliography & Recommended Resources

America's God and Country Encycl. of Quotations
by William J Federer
Copyright 1994, FAME Publishing, Inc.
The Bible Visual Resource Book
Copyright 1989, Regal Books
The Book of Psalms for Singing
Copyright 1973, Crown & Cross Publications
A Charlotte Mason Companion
by Karen Andreola
Copyright 1998, Charlotte Mason Research and Supply
A Christian Philosophy of Education
by Gordon H. Clark
Copyright 1988, The Trinity Foundation
Cultural Literacy:
What Every American Needs to Know
by E.E. Hirsch, Jr.
Copyright 1987, Houghton Millfin
Design Form U La
by Barbara Shelton
Copyright 1996, Homeschooling Seminars
Drawing Textbook
by Bruce McIntyre
Copyright 1988, Audio-Visual Drawing Program
Dumbing Us Down
by John Taylor Gatto
Copyright 1992, New Society Publishers
Education, Christianity, and the State
by Gresham Machen
Copyright 1995, The Trinity Foundation
A Family Guide to the Biblical Holidays
by Robin Scarlata and Linda Pierce
Copyright 1997, Family Christian Press

God & the History of Art
by Barry Stebbing
Copyright 1999, How Great Thou Art Publications
> ***Home Grown Kids***
> by Raymond and Dorothy Moore
> Copyright 1981, Hewitt Research Foundation

The Joyful Homeschooler
by Mary Hood
Copyright 1997, Ambleside Educational Press
> ***Language Arts the Easy Way***
> by Cindy Rushton
> Copyright 1998, Rushton Family Ministries

Lord of the Rings
by J.R.R. Tolkien
Copyright 1987, Houghton Mifflin Company
> ***Mathematicians are People, Too!***
> by Luetta Wilbert Reimer
> Copyright 1990, Pearson Learning

Relaxed Home School and ***Relaxed Record Keeping***
by Mary Hood
Copyright 1994 and 1996, Ambleside Educational Press
> ***Remodeling the Family***
> by Bernie A. Schock
> Copyright 1989, Wolgemuth and Hyatt Publishers

School Can Wait II
by Dr. Raymond & Dorothy Moore
Copyright 1982, The Moore Foundation
> ***The Simplicity of Homeschooling***
> by Vicky Goodchild
> Copyright 1997, HIS Publishing Company

What Do Our 17-Year-Olds Know?
by Diane Ravitch and Chester E. Finn, Jr.
Copyright 1987, Harper & Row, Publishers
> ***You Can Teach Your Child Successfully***
> by Ruth Beechick,
> Copyright 1992, Arrow Press

Appendix

I have included a copy of the way we generally do our high school transcripts. This is just a sample of what has worked for us over the years. There is nothing special or unique about it; you should do what works for your family! Mary Hood's book, *Relaxed Record Keeping* and Barbara Shelton's *Design Form U La* were very beneficial to me in the area of Record Keeping.

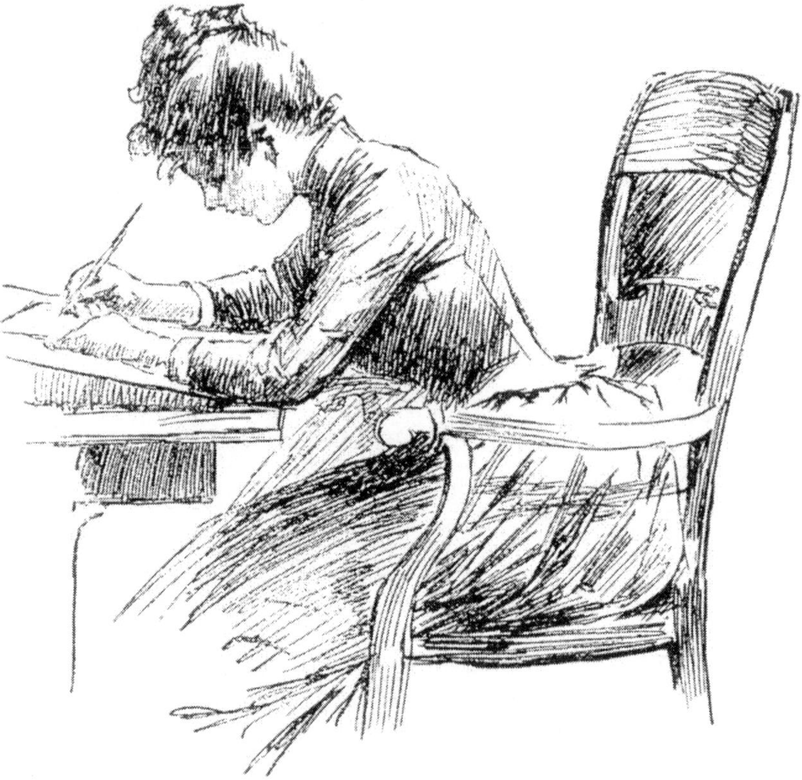

Student Name: _____ **JACOB INT'L ACADEMY**
Date of Birth: _____ Germany*El Paso, TX
Covers: Grades

OFFICIAL HIGH SCHOOL TRANSCRIPT

BIBLE
    Psalms   1   A
    Bible – O. T./N.T.   1   A

ENGLISH
    Drama   2   A
    Literature   ½   A
    Shakespeare   ½   A
    Composition   ½   B

FOREIGN LANGUAGE
    German   ½   A

HEALTH
    PE   1 ½   A

MATH
    Consumer Math   ½   A
    Algebra 1   1   B
    Logic   1   A
    Geometry   ½   B

MUSIC & ART
    Piano   2   A
    Vocal   ½   A
    Music Appreciation   ½   A
    Art Appreciation   ½   A

SCIENCE
    General Science   1   A
    Agriculture   1   A
    Biology (w/Lab)   1   A
    Animal Husbandry   2   A

SOCIAL STUDIES
    American History   1   A
    World History   1   A
    Civics (Youth Judicial)   2   A
    Government (Youth Leg)   2   A
    Architecture   ½   A

Administrator's Signature: _____
Parents:
Student Address:
Parents' Signatures: _____

Made in the USA
Charleston, SC
13 June 2012